A FRIEND FOR ALL SEASONS

BY
MARY PENDLEBURY

© Copyright 2004 Mary Pendlebury. All rights reserved.

No part of this publication may be reproduced, stored in a retrieval system, or transmitted, in any form or by any means, electronic, mechanical, photocopying, recording, or otherwise, without the written prior permission of the author.

Printed in Victoria, Canada

Note for Librarians: a cataloguing record for this book that includes Dewey Classification and US Library of Congress numbers is available from the National Library of Canada. The complete cataloguing record can be obtained from the National Library's online database at: www.nlc-bnc.ca/amicus/index-e.html

ISBN 14-120-1988-5

TRAFFORD

This book was published on-demand in cooperation with Trafford Publishing.
On-demand publishing is a unique process and service of making a book available for retail sale to the public taking advantage of on-demand manufacturing and Internet marketing. On-demand publishing includes promotions, retail sales, manufacturing, order fulfilment, accounting and collecting royalties on behalf of the author.

Suite 6E, 2333 Government St., Victoria, B.C. V8T 4P4, CANADA
Phone   250-383-6864   Toll-free   1-888-232-4444 (Canada & US)
Fax   250-383-6804   E-mail   sales@trafford.com
Web site www.trafford.com   TRAFFORD PUBLISHING IS A DIVISION OF TRAFFORD HOLDINGS LTD.
Trafford Catalogue #03-2466   www.trafford.com/robots/03-2466.html
10   9   8   7   6   5   4   3   2   1

God has brought so many people into my life and each one has left their own unique indeliable mark as time has gone by. He has brought me through so many trials and tribulations while at the same time blessing me in countless ways. One special way He has blessed me is with the gift of a true friend... A Friend For All Seasons.

With this in mind I dedicate this book to that vey speacial and unique person in my life. Diane this is for you. You have been an ongoing source of support, encouragement, laughter, joy and healing. Thank you for all of this and for that oh so amazing "one mind"

Table of Contents

Always	1
Soul Lace	2
The Gallery	3
Sorry	5
A Friend for all Seasons	6
Laughter	8
The Essence of Friendship	9
In the Garden	10
The Big 4-0	11
I'm Sorry	12
The Island	13
Rocking Chair	14
Rest Assured	16
Day Dreaming	17
Can You See It?	18
Angel Whispers	19
On Eagles Wings	20
Meet You at the Park	21
The Key	22
The Courage to BE	23
Run the Good Race	24
Hold On	26
Inside Out	28
Jenny's Secrets	31
Summer's Eve	43
Me and My Shadow	45
Life Projected	47
Stories My Mother Never Told Me	49
The Weeping Willow	51
Planting Mums	54
Angel Souls	57
The Old Wooden Swing	61
Medusa	64
A Day with Lance	66
Rebel Rouser	70

Not Just Another Cardio Class 72
Hot and Cold Flashes 74
House of Horrors 77
I've Lost My Mind 80
In the Trenches 82

ALWAYS

It's all the little things that are left unsaid
 Words for the greater things laying in wait
Validating the past left sorrowfully staid
 It's the leap of faith for which you are paid

Chance did knock and there it stayed
Passing through the womb of my soul
You lingered there 'til the torment subsided
Life indeed had taken its toll

Leaving not, in that womb you've resided
Igniting a spirit that was losing its breath
Quietly, so quietly you revived a life
The spirit grew wings and renounced its death

Onward and upward away from the strife
Like an angel of God you held out your hand
To beckon me forward into a living light
With subtle urging to take a stand

Retreat did I, from that darkest night
Life lessons we learned on the way
No longer alone to battle the past
I know in all things, here you will stay
Here I am, home at last

In gratitude true, you have helped me along
Understanding things left unsaid
For every quip you could turn into song
Your kindness ceaseless, your friendship my stead

In all things that mattered you stayed the course
Your loyalty treasured in unmeasured ways
In dreams to come, you've been the force
For this, I thank you.....ALWAYS

MARY PENDLEBURY

SOUL LACE

Deep inside is the lining of our life.
So simple and delicate, yet somehow complex.
It resembles the lace of a dress or doily in its elegance and grace.
While at the same lending itself to memories of something old.
Something put together with the workmanship of a true master craftsman.
After much time, patience and guidance the work is displayed.
It seems once put together the work is done.
But the master of this work knows the work has just begun.
For without occasional cleaning, this lace will gather dust and dirt, falling in ruin upon the floor.
Upon it gaze the eyes of the creator.
Those eyes hurt by the destruction and misuse.
Sometimes repairs can be made.
By washing the lace and carefully mending its tattered edges the lace is restored to the luster of its original shape.
Other times the damage so severe that the repairs once made sever in repeated misuse.
So too, we damage our souls after its careful creation by our Master.
So too, we must remember the special care that keeps the work intact.
This is sometimes hard because we know the delicacy of each woven thread.
What should be remembered at this time is the strength of the work as a whole.
The one, who made us, took great care and pride in what we would be.
So then, it is our special task to see the gift is given much care.
Then when we are once again in the company of its creator, few repairs will have to be made.
It is then that we shall have true soul lace (solace).

THE GALLERY

There is a gallery of pictures hanging in your mind.
 Each one marking a special place in time
 Each one reflecting pieces of you that when placed together form a life.
As you pause to regard each one, you are reminded of how far you have come.
Many pictures behind and more to come.

Some pictures titled "Loneliness" that could only be done in watercolor.
The water here were the tears that you shed.
When mixed in proper measure with hope and strength, gave vibrancy to each color.

Some marked both cornerstones and turning points and held the titles of "Learning on the Way" and "Foundations".
They are done in oil because they are the most indelible and take the longest time to cure.

Others done in charcoal or pencil, marking seeming insignificance for their simple place in line.
They to hold the essence of the day to day things that we often miss and fail to regard.
A part of you less colorful, but significant none the less.

There are many that are simply titled "Friend".
They share a similar feature...
Each one pictures you.
And to each is added a friend met along the way.
What each on holds is a memory of warmth and sharing.
But the eyes have been betrayed.
What's missing here that can't be shown is how in return you touched each one and changed a life for good.

You want to stay and linger a while but your eyes look ahead.

MARY PENDLEBURY

You see as you look down the long hall ahead, an assortment of canvasses yet to be fed.
The possibilities are endless and you scarce know where to start.
And the realization is suddenly stark.
At once you are both visitor and artist to the gallery of pictures hanging in your mind.
Pictures only painted when they are a step behind.
Beginnings to made with each step ahead.

SORRY

Sorry for all the times you have felt like the monkey in the middle.
Sorry for the times when everything and everyone seems out of reach except for the torrent of emotions that land on you.
Sorry for not making things better when I should, despite how I am feeling.
Sorry for all the times I seem to disappear and I can't ell you that I am not angry, just concerned or needing to sort things out.
Sorry for all the let downs you experience that leave you feeling like all that is left to do is "go with the flow".
Sorry things aren't better for you so you don't have to be referee especially when you need to disappear.
Sorry for every heartbreak and each time I have let you down.
Sorry for the silence when I don't know what to say or do.

MARY PENDLEBURY

A FRIEND FOR ALL SEASONS!

There are times when storms move in, taking us off balance.
It is a season of turmoil and seemingly unending strife.
It grabs hold and we feel it may never end.
Sometimes the season passes quickly, though it seems an eternity.
Other times it takes its time and we feel we can take no more.
We can ride it out or take shelter in a friend.

There are times for change and moving on.
This is the season of growth and for testing our strength — our courage to go on.
Sometimes our will bids us to wait, but that is only fear.
The temptation to stand still.
We can stand alone marking the passage of time by counting our regrets, or take the step and still accept, your friend is behind you all the way.

There are times of sunshine and perfect calm.
This is the season of contentment and joy.
The season of confidence, reassurance and pride.
In this too we are not alone.
The season only magnified when shared with a friend.

There are times that seem to bring us to a place lacking color and focus.
A time where we feel alone.
This is the season of solitude, restoration and re-evaluation.
A season of contemplation and searching the soul.
A season to be alone if only for a short while.
In the quiet, there waits your friend.
Knowing just how or when to step in.
Knowing sometimes it's better to listen.
Knowing and trusting that when the time is right you will let them back in.
The quietness shared in understanding when words cannot be found.

A FRIEND FOR ALL SEASONS

This I know is not just a friend for all seasons, but a friend for all times.
The friend that brings shelter in a storm.
The friend that brings encouragement, reassurance and joy.
The friend who hears, when nothing is said.
The explanation seems profound when the truth is simply a "friend for life".
The friend that brings life and shares life.
In many ways it is the friend who defines life.

MARY PENDLEBURY

LAUGHTER

The children are playing and having their fun.
Elated with life in the afternoon sun.
Simplicity is theirs, a rare treasure to behold.
Their cares are spun with threads of gold.

And there sits one off to the side.
Eyes with a sparkle, opened up wide.
Touching and feeling what was found on the ground.
Ants by the millions mound upon mound.

A skill lost by many in time through the ages,
The wonder and awe of these small sages.
Enraptured with life as it is with each day.
The laughter and beauty of a child at play

THE ESSENCE OF FRIENDSHIP

Understanding the silence of the unspoken word.
Healing emotions that may never be heard.
Endearing your heart with laughter that sings.
Sharing life's treasures that each day brings.

Being so near, though miles apart.
Sharing the comfort of friendship's heart.
One thought in your mind leaves you feeling alone.
Interrupted at once by a friend on the phone.

It's not about the big things that are easy to mark,
But rather the simplicities that light the spark.
Laughter unceasing long after you part.
Sorrow eased by the touch of a heart.

Somewhere to turn when things seem unreal.
A place to go when you need time to heal.
A bond created, cemented and earned.
A gift once given then freely returned.

MARY PENDLEBURY

IN THE GARDEN

Each time I go out to the garden I think of you.
Acquaintances many but true friends are few.
Each seed planted like one day in our life.
Each confidence shared like weeding our strife.

As I water each plant with the utmost of care.
I think of the laughter and tears we share.
And the promise and dreams of better days
Found in the warmth of the sun's bright rays.

It was down life's path we both were led.
Seedling plants needing to be nourished and fed.
Meeting at once in a place preordained.
Like plants in the ground washed by the rain.

In darkness of pain, in storms that pass by.
You are as the sun clearing the sky.
What started once as a simple seed.
Has rooted and grown in your every deed.

I thank you not in part but rather in whole.
Not just from my heart but also my soul.
For all that you give straight from your heart.
And for being my friend right from the start.

THE BIG 4-0

The years you've waited to get where you are,
Traveling emotions road long and far,
Patience and timing have come into line,
Comfort of heart and spirit aligned,
To you the cup of Joy is raised,
A whole new road ahead to blaze.

You've given friendship with the utmost care,
For many at once you have always been there,
With words of wisdom you have inspired,
Giving your best though weak and tired.
To you the cup of Friendship lifted,
A special woman uniquely gifted.

A lady of grace, class and passion,
No one else to win when it comes to fashion,
Not just ribbons buckles and bows,
Where it comes from no one knows
To you the cup of Life proclaimed,
The Lady of Fashion will hold the reign.

You have waited and waited for so many things,
Having nothing to do with money or rings,
Many hopes and dreams yet to be grasped,
So many things now left in the past,
The cup of Love never raised in part,
May it forever fill your precious heart.

Wishing for you on your special day,
Laughter and sunshine, joy that will stay,
Payment in kind for all that you give,
Wisdom and Courage for each day you live.
And now with Birthday Cup in Tow,
All the Best to you on the Big 4-0.

MARY PENDLEBURY

I'M SORRY

I'm sorry for the ache I put into your heart.
For messing things up right from the start.
I should have waited, listened, not been so quick to judge.
Then instead my pride stepped in and I refused to budge.

How do we begin again?
To soothe away the sorrow and heal all the pain.
To try again to build a trust.
I want to try, I'm willing to try, I must.

Please forgive me in my awkwardness and look into my eyes.
Reveal again the truth to me, I'll put away the lies.
I realize in my bitterness I made you come undone.
Please meet me in the middle so we can walk as one.

Help me to take down the walls that are keeping us apart.
Help me to strive to prevent another broken heart.
Help me to restore a love that has endured the years.
In doing so together we will overcome our fears.

THE ISLAND

I created an island.
An island in my mind.
I am the island.
A place to escape, a place to be free.
People were as sharp rocks, obstacles in my way.
They hurt… they are cutting.
Slowing the travel to my island oasis.

Rocks also help in building walls.
Why the walls?
The island would be so much more beautiful,
If the rocks were crushed to sand.
The most beautiful sand, around the most beautiful oasis.
But aren't sand and rock the same in varying degrees?
Though one is refined and one is course,
Both hold the capacity for cold and warmth.
Refinement comes with one's own perception.
What is an island if it were not surrounded by either?

MARY PENDLEBURY

ROCKING CHAIR

It happened time and time again,
Tears were falling like ceaseless rain.
How do you stop the pain of rejection?
How do comfort with loving protection?

A small piece of time refused a child in need.
It's not to the parent that the child should plead.
Please walk with me daddy, all the way home.
Don't leaving me waiting and standing alone.

Starring out the window dying inside,
Longing for love but instead pushed aside.
A little attention is all it would take.
It's not the child who made the mistake.

Comfort entered the room oh so slow.
Up in the rocking chair we would go.
Rocking, rocking, rocking away,
Soothing the sorrows that clouded the day.

Rocking, rocking, rocking away.
Sobs and tears finding their way.
Rocking, rocking, rocking away.
Cradled in comfort here we will stay.

Tears have blurred the blue skies above.
Comforted rocking 'til warmed by love.
Rocking, rocking, rocking away,
'Til slumber eases the pain of the day.

Hours had passed before the child awoke.
Still sitting and rocking not one word spoke.
Starring and wondering about the dream,
Of having a shoulder on which she could lean.

Rocking, rocking, rocking away.

A FRIEND FOR ALL SEASONS

Who will comfort me? Who would stay?
Rocking, rocking, rocking away.
Maybe they'll come another day.
Rocking, rocking, rocking away.

MARY PENDLEBURY

REST ASSURED

Rest assured that a new day will come.
The tempest eased that wrestles the heart.
That tomorrow arrives despite even one.
Inept am I to breathe life to its start.

I swallowed me pride and to God stepped aside.
Knowing not what would come to Him bent my ear.
I listened and heeded what was revealed deep inside.
He is with me each day and throughout every year.

He whispered in words known alone to my soul.
Assurance and comfort to me knew no bounds.
A love and forgiveness that where given in whole.
To each one lost and at once now been found.

I thanked Him each day for all that He gave.
My food and shelter – direction along the way.
Humbled, forgiven, no longer a slave.
Free to enjoy an eternity of days.

I rest assured that there will come a new day.
The tempest eased that wrestled my heart.
Humbled, forgiven, no longer a slave.
In His care forever, never to part.

DAY DREAMING

How enchanting it would be to hover in that dream state somewhere between being awake and asleep. A time to dream of how things need to be when you are at the end of your rope. It brings to mind a poem I read many years ago that was written by Harry Wadsworth Longfellow that reads as follows.

The Day is Done

The day is done, and the darkness falls from the wings of night,
As a feather is wafted from an eagle in his flight.
I see the lights of the village gleam through the rain and the mist.
A feeling of sadness comes over me that my soul cannot resist.
A feeling of sadness and longing, that is not akin to pain.
And resembles sorrow only as the mist resembles the rain.
Come, read to me some poem,
Some simple heartfelt lay,
That shall soothe this restless feeling
And banish the thoughts of day.

It touched me with its emotion and sent upon me thoughts of gratitude that are so often left unspoken. It's the gratitude that brings much peace when you are feeling so detached and lonely, until someone reaches out the hand of understanding that knows no words. And that is where your heart is when daydreaming of a solitude that seems so far from reach.

A restless soul is hard to ease. It's not of the intellect but of the heart where so few dare to tread. A restlessness that can be shattered with a single careless word when we are so absorbed in our own being to recognize the need of another. But equally so it is a restlessness that can give us the strength to persist in being because we know we aren't alone.

And always we return to that place that brings peace to our weary souls. It's the place we go to dream. It's the place we go when a child smiles. It's the place we go where understanding connects. And it's the place we go when someone let's us know we are not alone.

MARY PENDLEBURY

CAN YOU SEE IT?

They say it is hard if not impossible to believe in things you cannot see.
This is quite a paradox, more so if you are blind I suppose.
You see people, so you know they are real.
You see money, so know and say it is real along with all it can buy.
So then, if you see nothing does it mean nothing exists?
Does it mean there is no world?
Does it mean there are no sunsets or blue skies?
Perhaps the reality is that it is our eyes that make us blind.
What we see is what we want.
But it is what we cannot see that is perhaps what we truly need.
It is what we cannot see that is perhaps the greatest reality of all.
So too, it is what we cannot see that is the greatest truth of all.

ANGEL WHISPERS

Angel whispers touched my ears, soft as a baby's breath. My heart ached to hear more. My eyes strained in hopes that they would stay a little longer. I was waking up to a new day, saddened that the visit had to end. It was a long time since I felt the peace and reassurance of their presence. All that was left to me as I opened my eyes was the enormity of their presence yet the simplicity of their words. They were speaking to me, but why? I repeated the words over and over again trying to grasp the meaning. "It's almost time…. It's almost time"

God always answered my prayers, of that I was sure. I knew that this too was an answer to something. Lying there I strained to regain the simplest essence of what had just taken place. It was almost time – for what? There was so much I had prayed for and about and I was vaguely aware that I had just had a long conversation that now left my grasp until the time was right. Perhaps God just extended me His hand to pull me up out of my confusion and despair. Just reminding me that He was still there.

It had been to me as it was with so many others. Years of wondering in the desert of life. God fed me and quenched my thirst as needed. His grace and mercies endless. One thing remained and seemed unattended to until this moment. It was one of those things not seen by the eyes but by the soul. Not a broken heart of this world but a grieving spirit. A spirit broken not by the loneliness but rather the alone- ness. And so it was, that he sent His angels. They came to comfort and encourage. They came to say that He has heard the cry, mended the heart and freed the spirit. Once again I could hold on for all eternity because I knew He was at my side. All this confirmed with simple angel whispers that touched my ears.

MARY PENDLEBURY

ON EAGLES WINGS

As a child I dreamed of flying…of soaring through the air without a care. If only I could be an eagle. Their flight seems so effortless. Tipping their wings ever so slightly and cutting the air so sharply…turning swooping, soaring ever higher. I would watch in wonderment each time I saw one in flight. Inspired by how graceful they appeared. Intrigued at what an awesome view they had. A view that encompassed not only a spectacular overall look at what was around but simultaneously having an incredible eye for focused precision on their target below.

It was a lesson in life to look at the big picture while focusing on easily missed detail. A lesson of listening and watching until the time was right. A lesson in knowing when to stand alone. But as a child is was just as much about learning to fly for the sake of flying. Letting go of everything for the chance to be carried on the wind. A state of "being", not attainable while awake. A place of freedom in hours of slumber.

To be carried on the wings of an eagle. To feel the warmth of the sun. To be carried away from the chaos of the day. To appear so graceful. I would drift off to sleep or daydream while awake; I knew where I would go. I would be in the sky away from all the noise. I could be alone to enjoy the peace. I would return only when my weary heart was restored.

As a child I dreamed I could fly. As a child I went in dreams to places unseen. As a child on the wings of an eagle I learned to stand alone. Still there remains the feeling of flight. Though the wings are weary and the vision not as bright, still there remains the places of dreams. I close my eyes and the weight is lifted. Once again as a child, in the emotion of flight. Gone for the hours that extend over night. Raptured in solitude 'til dawn breaks it light.

MEET YOU AT THE PARK

When you are having "one of those days" I will meet you at the park. We will head to the swings and make the rest of the world disappear. With each glide through the air we can put more distance between "the day" and us. Just imagine the feel of the air on your face and the comfort of that pressure that leaves you feeling like you're suspended in flight and time. Imagine how far you would be able to jump when you have swung so high you could do a somersault over the top bar.

When you are having "one of those days" I will meet you at the park. A swing set for two so you won't be alone. We may be there for hours and without a care. You won't ever have to worry about others waiting their turn 'cause this park is located between our ears. When we can't physically go to they are, then just sit and imagine and soon we will be there. Flying higher and higher…sun on our faces…the breeze in our hair.

It's better than rocking chairs, hammocks and patio furniture. They will do in a pinch but the real thing can't be beat. One day we will sit on real swings and pass the time in that measured way. Each swing to-and-fro like a pendulum marking the tempo in the race to catch a bit of freedom. The simplicity of it all makes it seem rather silly. You and I both know there is just so much more that can't be explained. So keep in mind as the days go by that when you are having "one of those days", I will meet you at the park.

MARY PENDLEBURY

THE KEY

When one word can mean so much it's difficult to know where to begin. A key can relate to musical notes or a means to open or close a door or even used to denote a position or revelation. What they all have in common is that things need to be properly aligned to have things fall into place. It could be a key to open or close a door, or a key to resolving a problem. Many people use the expression "key to my heart". That is interesting.

To have the key to someone's heart, at some point undoubtedly means to have the key to their soul. As easily as this key can open you to vulnerability it can cause such pain and suffering that it destroys the lock. Damage that may never be repaired… at least not by the one who caused the damage. A key has to be as precise as the surgeon's scalpel to work properly and consistently. Each notch is significant and needed in it's own unique way.

The key itself may be love but each notch on the key can also be named. One notch is trust. Other notches would be gratitude, consideration, acceptance, compassion, respect, attention, appreciation, selflessness, honesty, time to listen, time to speak. If any of the notches are damaged the key may still work for a while but eventually if left unattended both the key and the locks are damaged beyond repair.

For every lock and every heart there is a key to fit. Sometimes it may seem lost and other times that special key is still being prepared. In either case another saying applies here as well…"The more keys a person has, the more responsibility they have as well". With this we must remember that the keys you hold can bring honor or disgrace; acceptance or rejection; or a place to call home. We always have choices to make. Our choices define not only how many keys we hold but whether we will keep them and all they have to open.

THE COURAGE TO BE

As I lay in bed waiting for eyes and mind to give in to the sleep that eluded me, my heart began to pray to God for all I needed to be. He has kept me in His care long before I drew my first breath. Silently I talked to Him about all that was to be. Silently I talked to Him about all that had already been. Silently I talked to Him and wondered where He would have me be. But most of all I prayed to Him for the courage to be.

The courage to be all I was meant to be.
The courage to be the friend I am needed to be.
The courage to fill a void where no one else dared to go.
I prayed to Him and listened still.
I prayed for my friends and all whom they loved.
I prayed for my family that I often find hard to love.

Still my mind wrestled with something beating at my brain.
The things I don't have answers for that elude me everyday.
I prayed for the courage, wisdom and strength that I need.
And as each night I go through the list, I finally remembered something I'd missed.

I prayed for much and begged for more. Forgetting all the while that He hears every word.
In my embarrassment and humbled once more, I prayed for the courage to accept all that He has offered me. And not the least of which I prayed for the faith I needed to believe in Him. I had believed Him for so long that I had taken for granted the one thing that has sustained me, not just my faith but that I could believe in Him and through Him.
And now I prayed again… not just for the courage to be but for the courage to allow Him to BE.

MARY PENDLEBURY

RUN THE GOOD RACE

With a clap of thunder and bolt of lightening as a shot being fired to start a race, God handed over the baton that began the race of life itself. To each is given a baton, which represents all that God has given us to go through life. Each going through life enduring the race, be it long in years or short on days. Only God knows how long we have.

The baton represents our gifts, our talents, His love and grace, strength and forgiveness. He gives us faith, courage, wisdom and a soul to know Him. All of this is packed into a baton, which is sealed with freewill. It is our choice how we use what He has given us. Some drop the baton through weariness, sorrow, hurt and discouragement. Some drop the baton because they feel that God doesn't really care. We forget that God never promised the race would be free of obstacles and hurdles, which we must overcome. Remembering always that just as He was with us in the beginning, so to will He be with us at the finish line. In all His glory and love, He awaits our return to Him.

Anyone who runs has heard about the runner's wall. This wall in our race, are the times we feel we are failing. We are weary and feel we can't go on. Many hit the wall and drop the baton, feeling it is too much to carry. We still must finish the race and come before God for an accounting. God never leaves us completely alone though at many times it may feel like He has. He gives us times of reflection, meditation, restoration and rest. A time to put things back into perspective. Some will demand answers they can't hear. Others, though weary, encounter other runners who will stop to encourage and to help replenish the one in need, for that is one of the gifts God has given him or her. Once again the wearied soul must chose again to either lay down and blame God and others for their lack of endurance, or look up to God in faith and realize they too can overcome the runner's wall.

The race goes on and those who endured conquer the wall. They see in the distance the end is drawing near. The finish line is drawing closer and the race has come to an end. And what will God say as we hand back to Him our life as it is? Will we be able to lay at His feet in all praise and glory to Him who has enabled us to stay the course? Will we be among the ones as in James 1:12 "Blessed is a man who perseveres under trial; for once he has been approved, he will receive the crown of life, which the Lord has promised to those who love Him"? Will God say to us in the end, as in Matthew 25:23 "Well done, good and faithful servant; thou hast been faithful over a few things: enter through into the joy of thy Lord." Will you "Be of good courage and He will strengthen your heart, all ye that hope in the Lord" (Ps 31:24)?

God alone knows the end. Yes, he has given us freewill, but what will we have to give back to Him as we cross the finish line and hand back to Him that precious baton of life that He hath given us? He has provided our every need. What shall we give Him in return? May we trust in the faith and love, grace and forgiveness given to us. Let not our will be done but that His will be done. Pray always that His will be our desire. When we can begin to do this then we will be strengthened to run the good race.

HOLD ON

Endeavoring to overcome loneliness and uncertainty seems often to be left to those who are forgotten. This is a great lie precipitated in the minds of those doing battle with day to day life. Feeling alone in their circumstances they do battle with themselves. How much energy could it take to breathe your next breath? How much more energy does it take to reach out to chance? Daring to believe that someone cares when it feels as though those around you are deaf and uncaring is like a shield with two handles. One handle held on one side held by the one in need, the other held from the reverse side by the one waiting for you to let go of the shield so they can help you put it aside and accept what their heart has to offer.

Where will we go from here? Shall we walk into the field of uncertainty or into the cave of fear? Put down the shield and let us walk into the field. The vast open field that is filled not only with life but with a vastness of possibilities only to be discovered when at once we take that first terrifying step. Breathe deep into your lungs the fresh air of freedom that comes with the courage to move on. Breathe deep into your lungs the breath of realization that comes with faith and hope. Dare to accept for yourself all that is good and strong. Lay down to the ground the weight from your back and from your heart that came from believing all that is in the past. The lies and deceptions that made you feel less than your own worst fears. And we shall wade through the water and stop to wash our eyes that they would see anew, removing the blindness created in our darkest days. May we now see ourselves as we really are in the light of new found friends. Those friends who are able to see the glimmer of things we thought were gone for good. Those things we thought no longer in our reach are being handed back to us as gifts to be accepted and cherished no longer tarnished by time gone by.

You are wondering what could possibly be returned to us that we would really want. It is the simple things that are so often taken for granted. They are our dreams from our childhood the ones left to collect the dust and shadows as we disappeared into our cocoon of survival. They are the attitudes of love, life, hope and respect that we surrendered along the way thinking we no longer had a right to their ownership in our own lives. They are the strength, courage and wisdom we held on to but in our blindness saw only as weakness, surrender and compromise that got us through another day. They are the simplest of things that give us joy. Those simple joys we had that seemed to be drowned by the thunderstorms that poured down on our lives. There may still be days that render dark clouds but in our new beginning we will be able to hold on and wait knowing the sun will return renewing our hearts and warming our souls.

What will you choose? Will it be a step back or a step forward? Knowing what has already passed, dare to step forward… cross the threshold and wander into the eternity of possibilities knowing that you never walk alone. Replacing the shield that once protected you with the friends that care. Only a friend can walk beside you freely. Anyone else would only hinder your walk, put potholes in your way, and discourage you from ever being more than they could dare to be themselves. Have courage, faith, hope and endurance. The rest of what you need shall come along the way as you meet more friends and accept for yourself all the things you have given to others in their journey through life. The best gift you can give yourself is a legacy to be left for those who follow. The willingness and ability to hold your head high accepting life at its best, expecting and receiving all the love, hope and respect you deserve, undaunted by the days that would cast their shadows. Daring to have faith when all seems hopeless. Daring to love when your comfort was once held in rejection. Daring to hold on when all reason tells you let go and fall into the past.

MARY PENDLEBURY

INSIDE-OUT

It was a day that made the birds sing. It was a day that made the trees come into full bloom. The air was warm and the breeze just light enough to lessen the heat of the sun. It was all this and more but only if you were someone else. It was all of this if only you could get outside of who you were expected to be.

There she was in the room all alone. Waiting for something she feared would never come. She was only six to those around her but inside she was and old woman. She surveyed the room looking for a kind eye, a warm touch, a comforting voice but that would not come. And so like so many times before, she sat alone marking the passage of time by observing the emptiness of the house that had so much. It was there where she dared to dream of things yet to come. At times she took comfort in being ignored. Then there were the times she screamed her hurt and loneliness only to have it land on deaf ears and stone cold hearts. It was the age of her wisdom that created the insistence that she hold out for…something, or someone that would acknowledge that she was more than and inconvenience to those around her. They didn't know that she had the heart of an artist, the soul of a musician, the mind of a scholar and philosopher but most of all the needs of a child.

So few dared to look past their expectations of her. So few dared to look into her eyes and see and eternity of living in the body of a six-year-old. What could she know or understand that could be of any use to anyone. It was that attitude that made her invisible. It was that arrogance that provided her with life's greatest classroom. It is those invisible children that have more depth than the deepest ocean. Each day she prayed for someone to hear her silent screams all the while so acutely aware that it could only matter if that person also spoke the same language. Not English or Polish or any other verbal language but the silent language that is only spoken by those who are invisible. The language spoken by those who choose to survive despite those around them who insist one be not only a shadow of their own weaknesses but also a means to vent their own rage at life being less than they could make it. The rage that comes from the fear of not being good enough.

    The years passed at a painfully slow pace but some things were changing. She started to meet others who spoke the silent language but they needed her more for a crutch and counselor but there was always a hint of that friendship. Each time the friendships were stronger and the crutches were weaker. Each time the language evolved to include and ever deeper sense of humor. She could see more clearly now that those childhood dreams could be realized. That she did in fact have a grip on the reality of what she needed. That it wasn't insane to think she could really be loved for who she was but there was a long way to go yet. Even though she could see a glimmer of hope she, at the same time, realized that she was still living life through the eyes and expectations of those people who didn't see or understand that old six-year-old. But this was all right at some level because she knew it was living incognito until it was safe to come out of hiding. It was safe until she was okay with reconnecting with the truth and wisdom of that six-year-old. She hadn't stopped believing she had just waited for the right time when her mind and age had come into alignment. She was the caterpillar in the cocoon waiting for the time to begin metamorphosing into herself. Yes, the years had passed slowly and with each passing year she wrapped herself slowly into the cocoon that had protected what was left of the artist, musician, scholar, philosopher and child. Most of the time it just felt like she was getting smaller but actually she was getting deeper.

    The day was approaching when everything would change. As in nature, there is a time for everything. The only way there is order is that each aspect of this creation is finely tuned to a clock set by the creator. The alarm went off for her when she realized that she had to complete the metamorphosis in order to live. That to just stay in the cocoon meant death. It was no coincidence that she was leaving her old life not only with the six year old that was holding out for this day but also the with the six year old she gave birth to in those years of struggle. It was a new life where she would once again learn to love, to live and trust and endeavor to

MARY PENDLEBURY

live life like it needed to be lived. She was inside-out. For the first time in her life she was with people who cherished who she was. She was with people who enjoyed life more because she was more real than anyone else they had ever known. With each day that passed she became more because she feared less. She trusted that what she dared to dream for in those early years had finally come into fruition. She was inside-out…. Exactly where she needed to be.

JENNY'S SECRETS

    Jenny lay on the couch allowing her mind to drift where it may. She had been thinking of so many people and situations. Suddenly, she was jolted from her thoughts as she reached for the phone that rang in her ears like a morning alarm. As she answered the phone she grinned from ear to ear as she heard that oh so familiar voice that brought her through so many years. It was Demi on the phone and they had much to talk about. They talked for at least two hours and the conversation was so timely that it fit right into where she had come from when the phone first rang. Jenny continued reminiscing over the conversation she had just had with Demi who lived a thousand miles away.

    As these thoughts passed through her mind she found herself sitting on the step by the door putting on her shoes. She was heading out the door to walk down the street to park by the lake. As she approached the park she could see three little girls had beat her to the swings. Not wanting to look overly anxious she continued to stroll along until she came to the bench not far from the swings and took a seat. She pretended to be focused on watching the waves come up on the beach but from the corner of her eye she watched the interaction between the three girls. She could hear the laughter and banter as they enjoyed the thrill of the swings. Then everything came to an abrupt stop. The two little blonde-haired girls looked at each other rather sheepishly and jumped off their swings first, leaving the dark-haired girl looking a little surprised and bewildered. As her swing slowed enough for her to jump off, she saw the other two girls skipping away and overheard one of the girls say to the other, "Come here, I want to tell you a secret." At this point Jenny turns to see the dark-haired girl standing sullenly alone by the swings while her friends whispered and giggled amongst themselves.

Jenny turned her head back to the lake. As the next wave washed to the shore so did a memory she had which was triggered by seeing the one little girl standing alone. She was remembering back to when she was about six years old which was about the same age as these little girls at the park. Suddenly she was back in the driveway of the home she had grown up in. She was looking at her sisters playing around her. They were both very blonde and she had dark hair. She remembered thinking, " Why had God made her so different that she didn't feel like she fit in her family?" She stood there staring into nothingness then found herself alone in the driveway; her sisters had run off to play elsewhere. Then she walked almost to the end of the driveway, looked up into the sun, the sky, and the puffy white clouds, and saw a few birds flying around. She stared and stared as the words welled up in her heart like tears to the eyes. When she could no longer hold back she continued to stare into the sky and prayed to God with her whole being. "Please God, send me my friend who is just like me". It wasn't a general request. She was pleading with God for someone she could already feel in her heart and she wanted her in her life right at that moment.

Another wave washed up on the shore and brought Jenny back to the park. As she looked around she realized that three girls were gone and she was alone in the park. She walked over to the swings, sat down on one facing the lake and began to swing back and forth while letting her feet drag on the ground. She looked into the sky remembering that old prayer she had prayed as a child and a silent "Thank you!" crossed her lips for the prayer that was answered twenty years after it was first uttered. The friend was the one who would be sitting beside her on the next swing even though she was a thousand miles away. Where had the time gone? It seemed like just yesterday and yet at the same time an eternity away. Jenny sat on the swing reminiscing a little more. With each swing back and forth as with each wave that came ashore, a memory would return similar in feeling to the one of the dark-haired little girl left standing alone as her friends bonded in their exchange of secrets. Jenny was like the shore. Each wave like a memory of the secrets she had kept to herself through the many years that had passed.

A FRIEND FOR ALL SEASONS

Jenny was in grade one when Sherry sat in the desk in front of her. She remembered Sherry's curly hair and the little ponytail scrunched up by the crown of her head even though her hair was not so very long. When she would laugh, it was always how she laughed that Jenny remembered. Her shoulders would touch her ears, her eyes would squint and she always covered her smile as she giggled like she was hiding from something she wasn't supposed to do. Then she knew why Sherry had come to mind. It was a day of humiliation that Jenny could relate to all too well. Memories may have been distorted in thinking Sherry had an ongoing problem but in actuality there were probably only a few incidents.

It was around lunchtime and we stayed at our desks for the ten to fifteen minutes we had to eat our lunch before we were sent out to play. Then it happened. Jenny was the first one to smell it because Sherry sat right in front of her. The class erupted – "What stinks?" Sherry turned beet red and froze in her seat. She had an accident in her pants. Tears began to fall slowly down Sherry's cheeks but still she would not move. The teacher excused the class and told us them that they could go out and play. Jenny wrapped up her lunch and took it outside with her. A short while later Sherry came out and headed straight over to sit by the church that was on the same property as the school. Jenny stood there and watched as Sherry slid down the wall and held her knees tight to her body as her head dropped into her knees. Jenny waited a moment in hesitation still holding her lunch in her hand. Slowly she made her way over to Sherry and sat down beside her. There was still a residual bit of smell but Jenny ignored this as she handed Sherry half of her bologna sandwich and they sat there in silence until the bell rang to go back to class. Before the bell rang Jenny sat with Sherry in quiet understanding as she remembered what happened to her when she was in kindergarten. She wanted to tell Sherry but kept her secret to herself.

When Jenny was in kindergarten her mother sent her to school sick with a note she was to hand to her teacher. The note read: "Please excuse Jenny to use the washroom as she has diarrhea today." Jenny knew the essence of the note because she had pleaded with her mother not to write it. The teacher said nothing until the class was in their morning circle that began each day. The rule was that if you needed to be excused you had to raise your hand and ask permission to go and use the washroom. The teacher turned to look at Jenny and in a soft voice that to Jenny sounded like and announcement over the P.A. system…. "If you need to go to the washroom today it will be all right if you just go without raising your hand." At one point in the day Jenny was in the washroom so long that the teacher came in to see if she was all right. Jenny felt the heat of embarrassment rush into her face as she said she was all right. She knew she was not done and she was starting to fear she would run out of toilet paper. She finally managed to return to the classroom trying desperately to keep her embarrassment at bay.

    Another wave hit the shore and the memories kept rolling in with each one. Still in thought as the swing went back and forth, Jenny thought of Rebecca who was in her class in grade three. She had thought of Rebecca, her sister Helen and their mother many times over the years but one incident in particular stood out the most in her mind. It was Rebecca's birthday party. Jenny and her sister were invited and gladly attended. It seemed that there should have been more people there for such a special occasion. Jenny could only remember sitting at the picnic table with Rebecca, Helen, their mother, Jenny's sister and perhaps one other child. Everyone seemed a little nervous because everyone at the table was so shy. Perhaps the exception here would be Jenny's sister who tried to break the ice by asking a question. It may have been something about where their father was. Jenny kicked her sister under the table as if to tell her to shut up. Jenny felt there were many secrets in this home and with that understanding tried to keep the conversation less intrusive. This was a day that gave Jenny a better understanding that came out of the unspoken things in her own home. She realized that Rebecca was part of a low-income single parent home at a time when you didn't talk about those things or "those kind of people". She understood how important it was at that moment that she and her sister were allowed to come to this birthday party and how much it meant to Rebecca and her family.

    Jenny accepted the situation for what it was; never revealing to anyone how much she could identify with this family. Her mother always said it was wrong to discuss other people's business. She implicitly knew that this also meant you never discussed what was happening in your own home. She kept it all inside. When Jenny and her sister arrived home from the party they told everyone what a great time they had and the day went on. At some point later in the day, Jenny was becoming overwhelmed with emotion. In her house the only really acceptable expression of emotion had to come in the form of humour, laughter and happiness. Jenny didn't know what to do. She realized that the house was kind of quiet as everyone was outside playing. She needed somewhere to be alone. Almost as if she were in a trance she found herself ascending the stairs that led to her bedroom. She opened the door to the closet, stepped inside this very small space and closed the door behind her. She then slid down the wall, curled her knees up, and buried her face into her arms, which she had crossed over her knees and wept. She wept for Rebecca and her family and she wept for all the things she was not allowed to express.

    For most of her life Jenny never felt like a child even though there were happy times, there was a loneliness that burdened her soul. She remembered how she always felt responsible for the kids who were being ignored as if to somehow, perhaps, take care of herself at the same time. She remembered standing alone on the playground at school many times. Sometimes she thought about that friend she so longed to meet. Then she would see someone else out there that could take her away from that. In grade four, there was Maureen. Jenny hated the whispers she heard in class about how bad Maureen smelled and that the perfume she wore only made matters worse. Before she knew it, she and Maureen were talking and having a great time. Maureen asked Jenny if she would be allowed to come to the Fair that would be in town on the weekend. Jenny was allowed to go and meet Maureen there as they had planned. She went to pay for some tickets only to find out that she would not be allowed to pay for anything because she was there as Maureen's guest. As it turned out Maureen's family ran many of the rides and concession booths that were there. Jenny didn't know what to do about this and felt very guilty receiving such a gift. She was always expected earn everything. When the shock wore off she came to the realization that in some small way this was Maureen's way of thanking her because she was a friend who wasn't using her. Maureen moved after that year and Jenny never knew where she went. Years later, Jenny was walking into town and saw a truck pull up beside her. As she turned to look she heard a voice say "I knew that was you, I could tell that walk a mile away!" It was Maureen. Jenny was so happy to see her again and gladly accepted the ride. They talked for a while as they reached her destination. Jenny told Maureen how great it was to see her again and hoped they would meet again sometime and have a better chance to talk some more.

There was another person that came to mind as Jenny was on that swing. It was Demi at a time long before they ever met. It was long before Jenny ever knew her name or saw her face. She was remembering a class trip to Niagara Falls when she was in grade six. She was excited about going on the trip and made sure she brought her camera to take pictures. When her class arrived at the Falls, Jenny began a search that kicked in as if she was on automatic pilot. She had a sense of expectation that her friend was close by. Maybe today would be the day God was going to let her meet that friend she had prayed for. She was distracted all day long and feeling unimpressed but the sites she and her class had come to see. She searched every face and looked carefully at each person she saw sitting on a bench. Each time one of her friends remarked to her about something they had just seen or where they were going next, Jenny replied half-heartedly and with a sense that she was being interrupted from something far more important. The day was coming to a close and everyone was getting on the bus. Jenny just kept looking around like she had just left her best friend behind and who was going to take care of her. She didn't dare tell anyone, not even her best friend at the time that she had spent the day looking for someone she hadn't met. It wasn't until years later Jenny learned that Demi had

A FRIEND FOR ALL SEASONS

grown up in Niagara Falls.... Her best friend was living half an hour away but in grade six it was a world away. That day in the park sitting on the swing was different. Demi may have been physically a thousand miles away but at the same time she was sitting right beside Jenny enjoying the escape from the day.

Many people had come and gone in Jenny's life; each one left their mark in a multitude of ways. So many passed through her mind like the wind in her hair as she flew through the air on that swing in the park. She didn't just remember those with whom she had shared a bond of secrets left unspoken. She remembered also the laughter she shared with her friend Karen. They were alike in so many ways and could make each other laugh until they cried or peed their pants, whichever came first. She would have to remember to call Karen when she arrived home from the park, just to say hello and she how she was doing. Jenny wasn't really ready to leave just yet; she had to push that swing to the limit to catch a piece of that freedom, flight and separation from the cares of the day. She looked to the sky and the setting sun and held out to the very last moment as the swing went through its pendulum run. Then ever so slowly the tempo did wane. As she had done when she began, she sat on the swing until her feet dragged on the ground, reluctant to leave though knowing there would be another day to return to catch the sun.

Jenny started the return walk home feeling better for the experience and the short trip through time, remembering so many who had passed through her life. She decided to take a different route home from the one that had originally brought her to the park. As she walked along she took in the sites with a revived appreciation for what was around her. About a block from her home her foot kicked something and she looked down to see what it was. She looked down to find a key, picked it up and let the shape melt into her hand as she felt the ridges while wondering about who may have lost it and if it was the key to someone's house. She played with the idea for a while then as she often did with Demi her mind she went into a familiar mode. Jenny and Demi would often take one object, word or idea and sort of look at it from a multi- dimensional point of view. This was very much like the process that would lead them into long drawn out scenarios that would leave them laughing until they cried. They would be operating almost as one mind taking a simple concept, build upon it and turn it into a myriad of ideas and pictures that seemed endless. That was just one more thing that made Demi such a uniquely special friend. Demi was a definitely an important key in her life.

Yes, a key could mean so much…. That was the last thing on Jenny's mind as she drifted off to sleep that night. It would be, as she slept, that all illusive key that opened a door in her dreams to a past she had wanted to put out of her mind. She awoke about 3:00am with the urgency to capture what she had been dreaming. It was something to do with shadows and dragons. She had to write it down so she could tell Demi about it. As she wrote she filled in more detail trying first to explain things to herself. She started writing slowly at first and then it was as if her pen in hand could not race across the page at the speed of her mind. When she had finished writing she stopped to read back to herself what she had written.

She was very taken back at first but it made her realize that it was like a culmination of bigger fears and secrets that lay beneath the surface of what she had written. She had gone through a period of flashbacks. She could almost feel the same level of anxiety she felt when she was about eighteen months old. The man said he was taking her upstairs to change her diaper. The family had company over that day. She remembers because everyone was sitting in the living room. The man picked her up and as they ascended each step her anxiety grew. She was almost crying by the time they were at the top of the stairs. To the left at the top of the stairs was a small bedroom. In the bedroom was the old Singer sewing machine that doubled as a change table. Jenny was becoming more panicky, she knew something was wrong. The man undid her diaper but didn't change it. She could feel him touching her and she didn't like it. The next thing she remembers was the searing pain she felt. It went from her groin area to the top of her head. She was kicking, screaming and crying with everything she had in her and could feel the heat of rage in her face. The man held her down then did her diaper back up and took her back down stairs with some comment about accidentally pricking her with the pin from her diaper. Since she was only about eighteen months old and not yet talking so was unable to scream to everyone in that room that it was not a pin that pierced her skin but rather a demon that pierced her soul.

Over the next nineteen years she had lost count of the number of times she had been mentally, emotionally or sexually abused in one form or another. As in her dream about shadows and dragons, she found a way to survive and overcome. Jenny knew at the same time that Demi was out there fighting her battles on her own. She knew instinctively, like one who was separated from their identical twin that Demi had stopped counting the number of times her soul had been pierced by the people in her life. Jenny half smiled to herself as she saw herself and Demi as dragon slayers. There was one incident in particular that seemed to really certify her as a dragon slayer but it took a number of years to accomplish. It began when she was six years old.

Jenny was walking home from church. It was about a mile from her home. She walked down the hill that brought her to a small bridge that crossed a creek. When she was about half way across the bridge she stopped. It was like something was holding her back. She turned towards the creek and watched the water rush over the rocks and under the bridge. She didn't know how long she had been standing there doing battle in her mind. Her eyes went from the creek to the path, a short cut she and her brothers, sisters, and friends would often take. The path ran along the creek then up an embankment that came out at a variety store. She had the distinct feeling she shouldn't take the short cut that day but didn't know why. She was rationalizing it in her head and at the same time could hear those mocking voices of her brothers telling her not to be a baby – we always go this way.

Jenny gave into the mocking voices of her brothers and started walking towards the path but something didn't feel right. Her stomach was starting to turn more and more as she walked down the path. She continued along in her trepidation and as she came to a bend in the path the answer was clear. There sitting on a rock with stick in hand looking at her with expectation was Wayne. It was Wayne, who years back had held a knife to the neck of her oldest brother. Jenny stood frozen in her tracks as she heard Wayne's voice saying, "What cha got under there?" "Gonna show me what you got?" As he said the words in the tone of a maniac he poked and prodded at Jenny with a stick, lifting her skirt and hooking her underpants. She tried to stay focused. She looked down and saw a rock and thought to herself – if I can get that rock and pick it up, I could hit him with it and get away. She sort of started to put her plan into action then realized that Wayne must have realized what was going through her head. She started to move. The next thing she could remember when she "came to" was running up the hill that would take her to the road by the store. She could hear Wayne chasing her through the woods laughing the laugh of a completely insane person. Jenny was crying and trying to make her way up the hill even though she kept slipping. She remembered getting to the top of the hill but didn't know how she got home. Her mind had blanked out again.

    She remembers the whispers at home. Her parents wondering what to do about the situation and then deciding to do nothing. It was suggested in the whispers that "she" wouldn't remember it when she grew up. They would pretend nothing had happened. So once again she was left to sort things out on her own. She fought with her mother numerous times after that over having to wear a dress or skirt. If her mother won so did Jenny. She would put on the skirt or dress but not without wearing a pair of pants at the same time. This went on for some years and it got to the point where she wouldn't wear a dress or skirt for anything.

    When Jenny was about ten years old she had built up quite a bit of rage and guilt over the whole incident that she had kept to herself. That changed drastically one day while she was sitting out on the front lawn by herself just thinking. She had been there for some time when she noticed out of the corner of her eye someone walking up the street towards her. She turned her head and saw Wayne. Something inside her took hold as their eyes met and she saw that evil smirk on Wayne's face. She was holding her ground. She stared him down accusingly as he walked passed her and held his eyes. Suddenly she could see in his face a recognition and knew that he knew what her eyes where saying. She saw in his eyes for a split second that he had flinched. This six-foot tall man, big and evil had flinched as a 10-year-old stared him down. As he passed her, she let her eyes burn into the back of him and he must have felt it because he turned his head back for just a peek and could see that Jenny wasn't running scared. She had slain the dragon on some level and never saw Wayne again. It didn't heal all the scars but to her it was a victory that she would no longer be his victim.

Demi too had become a dragon slayer in her own right. She and Jenny would share many battle stories and in the process acknowledge one another for who they really were separate from whom they were expected to be. So too, would they learn to separate themselves from the toxic people and situations in their lives as together they traveled the road of healing, no longer having to fight alone. It takes a great deal of courage to choose to survive and each one felt that it was not God alone who got them through but the awareness deep in their souls that other existed. It was as if God had connected their souls as another means for them to hold out for something that wouldn't come until they were adults. They survived the insults, lies, secrets, betrayals and most importantly they survived having to live as functions in other peoples lives. Neither Demi nor Jenny was allowed to live as the children and people they should have been allowed to be. It was for this reason that in many ways they learned to became invisible so that on some level they could be invincible until it was time for them to meet and together breakdown the walls that were guarding their souls.

Yes, Demi was a dragon slayer as well. This woman who was so intelligent, caring, insightful and beautiful had that mark of silence that could only be truly recognized by someone else who had come off a similar battle field with the essence of their "being" just barely intact. Jenny was right back where she had started…remembering their conversations and how much they had shared, healed and grown over the years. She was so appreciative of all they had been through together. It wasn't just the difficult times but just as importantly it was the intense joy, laughter and practical jokes that spotted the landscape of their own little world. Some of which was shared with others but most was savored in a simple look that reminded them that so many times words were never needed.

SUMMER'S EVE

Docile trees spotted the landscape. The winter had settled in seemingly before fall had gotten underway. Leaves still lay lifeless on the ground. A reminder that fall had in fact passed and the snow of winter had left its weighted mark on the land. The snow could still be seen in a few places but it too was becoming history. The chill in the air left an ache in my bones. It was that kind of ache that seems only to be soothed by the warmth of summer.

I needed this time to walk and think. To sort out the thoughts that settled in my head. There had been so many moves that it seemed the likelihood of settling was a probable as stopping the seasons from changing. It was a feeling like all those times when you are afraid to enjoy something because something always came along to cast a shadow over the pleasure. I had spent so much time trying to pace myself to stave off the panic that was creeping up on me. Just like the walk this day, the ache was settling into my bones and I feared it would never go away. And then I reminded myself…it's like taking a walk…you can only take one step at a time or you trip yourself up.

I was so caught up in my thoughts that I failed to see that the sun was actually out and it was attempting to bring me warmth. There was also a warmth in me I was afraid to feel. I was moving to where there were people who wanted me. I was moving to a place where the cold ache of winter wouldn't settle in my bones. I was not just moving away but moving on. The ache was not from the cold of the air so much as it was the cold of my family. I was being given the chance to start again where no one knew me. Perhaps it was as much about starting for the first time in my life to do something for me.

It seemed so trivial, when I began my walk everything around me was lacking color. It was like being in a really bad black and white movie. Now as I sat on the bench to take a breath and soak in not only the sun but also the realization that the aching inside of me was beginning to ease a bit. I stared at the sky, silently asking for all the help I needed. The sky was an amazing blue and the clouds, though few, had an elegance ever changing by the whispering breeze.

    I leaned over resting my elbows on my knees. The grass was attempting to turn green in places. The children on the swings were screaming to go higher. Just to the right of my feet I looked intently to see a brave little crocus daring summer to arrive as it poked it's head up through the rich moist soil. As I looked around to see more crocuses with the same daring intent, it served to remind me that it was indeed summer's eve. A time for change and a new life to begin. It was a time to trust that the summer's warmth would wash in on the heals of spring showers.

    My days were not done on this afternoon and I had only to continue to take a single step at a time. Things would go on changing, one day into the next. There was a lifetime of decisions that still had to be met but for today one had been made. I would make the move and stay the course. I need only make the first step before I could ever know what would come next. I would never be settled until I was free to move ahead without fear. I would move forward with purpose just as each new season did. Today it is summer's eve. Tomorrow will be out of my reach until the sun had set and time eased me into a new set of possibilities. All I need will come to me in time. Until then, I will be content in knowing that there will always be a place to go where the sun is shinning and it's warmth will ease the ache in my heart and in my bones.

A FRIEND FOR ALL SEASONS

ME AND MY SHADOW

There have been times in my life that I have lived life in my shadow. A part of me that casts a reflection of the real me. It's not unlike a reflection in a pool of water. It isn't something I can grab without distorting both myself and the image I reflect. Each move creates a different picture. There is a person everyone else sees then there is me, left alone at times, to accept or reject what I don't want to see. A shadow is created by light being blocked. My shadow, to me, hasn't just been that something intangible. At times if has followed me like and anchor. It has been my doubts and fears.

The shadow cast at dawn is not as dark. It is ever changing 'til the sun reaches its final destination in the sky. The shadow cast at dawn has more hope for days ahead. But the shadow cast at dusk is darker like the days that are filled with confusion and unrest. A reminder of the fear of change.

It may seem odd to use the picture of a shadow to understand uncertainty. It may seem odd but then again sometimes my fears are as illusive as the shadow I cast. I have laughed at times when I have heard the saying "She's afraid of her own shadow". It is about being just as afraid of the things I want to change as I am of the things that aren't for me to change. Growing up in a dysfunctional family is a perfect example. The shadow of living up to the expectations that you were to behave as an adult while at the same time fearing the child you were suppose to be. The shadow of expressing your hopes and fears. The shadow that stays to one side as you attempt to function according to what you perceived was expected of you at an given time from any given person or situation.

I saw another shadow just recently that froze me in my tracks only because I had not expected to see it. I was so busy with everyone else that I didn't recognize who I was. I spent so much time making sure everyone else was all right that I hadn't seen that my shadow was larger than me. I have always been independent. That was understandable. I have always been available to those around me which encouraged me and strengthened me. That may seem like a good thing but at that moment I realized that it had become my shadow that was functioning and not really me.

The shadow here was also my fear. The fear of becoming invisible to me. I had to decide if I "would" rather than "could" take care of myself. It's different than being independent it means BEING. That wasn't a new concept it was just a new approach. Now I would have to take everything I have said and done for others and decide if I could accept the same for myself. The battle began. I have deceived myself into believing I was existing but in actuality was only surviving. The battle was about feeling Vs coping; loving Vs leaning on something that only resembled love; accepting what was right for me Vs accepting what others have decided was right for me.

It has at various times been difficult for me to admit what was best for me because that meant feeling something real – good or bad – it meant acknowledging my own needs rather than the needs of others. It was that shadow of dusk that was the darkest, scariest place to go. It had always been forbidden. Would I open myself up to the fear of rejection or add another brick to the wall that my shadow had been building for years? Would I embrace my hopes and dreams (try to revive them) or would my shadow steal from me my last once of strength?

It was not the sun casting the shadows that followed me. It was the dragons in the path of my life who with their fiery breath illuminated the area around me casting false shadows. I would slay the dragons and lay them to rest. Look into the sun and take in the warmth of things that bring life. I will turn toward life having faced the dragons and laid them to rest. Once again the shadows I cast will be as they should be, like the sundial of life marking time in relation to the sun's warmth on my face.

A FRIEND FOR ALL SEASONS

LIFE PROJECTED

She came down the stairs and stepped back 30 years as she gazed ahead. Staring at a class of 10 and 11 year-old children doing a class project for math. They were learning percentages and the teacher decided to incorporate a little project to make the lesson more tangible. Each child would step into the line and proceed to the front of the class. As each one arrived at the front of the classroom they would be weighed and a measurement taken for their height. From there they would make charts and show what percentage of the children were over or under a given height and weight. Obviously this would be a very stressful endeavor for those in the class who had for years been teased about their physical attributes.

It was her turn now and with clenched teeth she stepped on the scale and then proceeded to the area where she would be measured for her height. She could feel the redness in her face reaching fever pitch as she waited for the taunting to start. And then she heard the unexpected. "Hey, that's amazing you and I are the exact same weight and height". "We are the only two in the class that are the exact same". She looked up in astonishment. It was one of the most popular girls in her class talking to her. How could that be that they were the exact same height and weight? She was the fat kid and this other girl was the bean- pole. Someone had obviously made a mistake. Everyone must be blind not to see how different she looked. Her family had always told her how fat she was and surely her family wouldn't lie about that. The memory played over and over in her head like a broken record repeating that phrase over and over again… "Hey, we're the exact same… exact same… exact same…" To this day it didn't matter that one of the most popular girls in class had acknowledged her. She was stuck in the injustice of the situation. Someone had lied or made a mistake and one day someone would wake up to reality and tell the whole world about that one incident and ruin her life for good.

MARY PENDLEBURY

She was still that fat little kid waiting for the ridicule to be spoken aloud instead hearing the hushed whispers that replayed the injustice of that long lost day. She didn't know how long she had been away but startled back to reality as she heard the voice behind her saying… "Hey droopy drawers, if you loose any more weight I am going to start buying you those draw string pants from that old lady". It was her son. At ten years of age he was developing quite a sense of humor. "Haaa ha!"… She had turned slightly to her left and looked around as he made his way to the kitchen. "She knew that what he had said was "droopy drawers" but what she heard was "baggy butt". With her son out of sight she had to take one more look. She was right and the mirror couldn't lie. At five- foot- seven and 120 lb. she would forever be the short little fat kid. Life projected in a mirror image that was more than thirty years old. Life projected in a mirror, not seeing what was right in front of her but rather all that was reflected from the past. Those things that don't go away because she has stepped away from the mirror because they are just as those objects that are in line with the mirror everyday until the room is rearranged and the view is different. Life projected not by the mirror but rather the mind's eye.

A FRIEND FOR ALL SEASONS

STORIES MY MOTHER NEVER TOLD ME

As children many were told stories or had someone read to them before they fell off to sleep. A sort of ritual to help calm away the worries of the day. Often they were told fairy tales, stories of how things might be to encourage and hopefully give a child sweet dreams. My mother wasn't much for that. She preferred to tell us things like "Don't ever hit your mother or when you die your hand will be sticking out of your grave and then everyone will know that you hit your mother". Other times it would be things like… "When I was young daddy use to check to see if we had gone to church by asking us to repeat the sermon from that day." She taught us to pray and taught us the Ten Commandments. Then there were the days that were filled with things like… "How do you think the other person felt when you did that, how would you like someone to do that to you."… "God gave you good instincts, now use them".

The list of things could go on and on none of which were really stories. The things we were to learn were taught mostly by example. My mother never really told many stories but she taught me to read. To look at a person and not through them. Like the time we were in the city and saw an elderly man obviously drunk and living on the street. It was painful to watch this man picking through a garbage can looking for something to eat. Ever mindful that each person no matter his or her circumstances had a right to dignity, my mother approached the man and dropped a five-dollar bill close to him. Saying hello to the man she then said "Excuse me sir, it this what you are looking for, I think this must have fallen out your pocket." The man looked at her and wasn't sure what to say but his eyes said thank you in a million ways that words would never adequately express.   That was one of my early lessons in learning to read. She taught me the importance of looking into some ones eyes to see their soul. It was the real life version of not judging a book by its cover. Perhaps instead the man was severely dehydrated and hungry rather than drunk. That was the benefit of the doubt my mother was going to give this man. As we walked away she held my arm tightly and told me not to turn around so that we wouldn't embarrass this human being in need. My mother taught me that seeing has less to do with looking and more to do with observing.

Another aspect of story telling is hearing. Again the stories came from life. My mother had a real of knack for meeting immigrants and making them feel like they had lived here all their lives. As we walked back from town one day we stopped to talk to a man working in his garden. " Oh what a wonderful garden you have, I can see that it is very special to you and you have taken such care with it". The man hesitant at first did his best make himself understood. Pleased by the compliment he tried to tell us more in his very broken English. We came to learn that he and his wife had come here from Poland. Over the next several years we visited them often. I would go to visit them on my own and strain my ears to understand everything this man had to say. My brother wanted to come with me to visit one day because he had been hearing so much about this wonderful man and his wife. Trying valiantly to make conversation with this man my brother said the wrong thing. Next thing he heard was "You go home, not make fun with me" I pleaded with the man saying that my brother just didn't understand and he wasn't making fun of him. Everything was made right with "Fine, you stay not talk" It was times like this that entrenched what my mother wanted us to know. It is more about hearing someone and less about just listening to them.

No, my mother wasn't much for story telling she was more about life living. The stories wouldn't be about the white picket fence or the knight in shining armor, they would be about learning to read. Seeing people and situations not by merely looking but by observing. Understanding people and situations not by merely listening but by hearing. There were so many stories my mother never told me but she taught me how to read.

THE WEEPING WILLOW

When I was twelve I made a trip to Newfoundland with my mother to attend a cousin's wedding. There was really only one thing that impacted me for life on this trip and it had nothing to do with the wedding. One day we entered a church to attend the service. This was a very large church and I remember on the altar there was a glass coffin. I think it was suppose to be Christ in there reminding us that He had died for our sins. I thought to myself – how strange to have something like this on an altar especially since Christ had risen. We sat in the front row and the service began. I remember having a strange feeling of expectancy like someone waiting for company to arrive.

Part way through the service the feeling intensified and something drew my attention to the back of the church. It was a very long way to the back. Suddenly I saw a man walking up the aisle. His clothing was very worn and he walked with hat in hand, straight down the middle of the aisle. I know everyone was thinking…" How dare this bum come in here – late no less – and trying to find a seat at the front."

To this day I cannot tell you what the man looked like except that it was very apparent that he had lived a hard life. Looking like he may have been in his late fifties or perhaps sixty he may only have been in his forties. My instincts told me something was very different here. My mother tugged on my arm to get me to face forward but I could not take my eyes from him. He proceeded up the aisle passed the first row of seats and on he went up to the glass coffin. I could hear the murmuring in the church and vaguely remember a pause in the sermon. I was transfixed as I watched this man fall to his knees. At first there were silent pleas then the man continued - He wept out loud pleading for forgiveness over and over again weeping uncontrollably. I thought my soul would implode. I wanted to go and stand next to him but something held me in my place. This man had not come to church he had come to God. He came up that long aisle not out of courage but with hat in hand and tattered clothes that reflected the condition of his soul, this man came in humility. This man came to be forgiven.

   The years would pass and this experience clung to me as rigidly as what was about to come next. I awoke with a jolt from a dream that wasn't. It was a command. I saw him sitting on the side of his bed deciding life or death. I had spoken t him many times over the past several months and saw him drowning in a depression that was about to engulf him. What was I to do? I was sitting now on the side of my bed in a state of fear and indecision. "Why me?" but the command was repeated. "Go, now and speak to Earl he is in trouble". " I was more afraid of what I would say to his mother when she answered the door at 3:00 am - Why would I have to speak to Earl at 3:00 a.m. I spent so much time debating the issue I never walked the four blocks to Earl's house. Something that would have taken ten minutes of my time - delivering a simple message that would never be received. I went back to sleep.

   Morning came in more ways than one. The new day brought the news that Earl had taken a gun into his hands and in a split second a life was gone for good. For years I heard the echo of that gun going off. For years I heard the phrase…." Just go and tell him that I love him and I will bring him through the darkness". I had been delivering mail for over a year. I used to see Earl a number of times on whichever route I was assigned to for that day. Then, God had assigned me to make a priority delivery that would have His signature on it. They say the mail is delivered through rain, snow, sleet and hail. I was to deliver a message that was to calm a storm and failed to deliver not due to weather but rather fear.

   The world is so wrought with strife. Babies are raped, children are molested, human beings are beaten beyond recognition physically, mentally and emotionally for no justifiable reason. People of all ages filled with sorrows and horrors that the mind cannot comprehend. Every night before I sleep and even through the day. I pray for each and every person God has brought into my life. I pray for their comfort, for God to heal the sorrows of their soul as well as the easing of the worries that each day brings. I know He cares for each and everyone and will attend to every need.

    As I sleep He comforts me and brings me to a dream. I walked a path lined with trees each one holding its own explicit beauty. As I walked along I took in the smells of the rich earth, the fresh air and budding trees. I listened to the birds chatter and sing as I continued down the path. I knew this was the place that I would stop to rest. I found myself beneath a willow tree that seemed quite out of place. I looked at it in wonderment and listened while He spoke to me. This willow looked like so many others. It had a strong trunk that reached to the sky. Branches in abundance seemed laden with burdens as they drooped sorrowfully toward the ground. And He spoke to me… The willow's trunk is His Son Christ with roots grounded firmly and deeply in the Father. Each branch it bears as each single leaf was to Him like the cares of the world and each prayer I prayed. It seemed the tree was burden filled, weeping for the lost, weeping for the forgotten. This was only part of it. Yes, the tree appeared heavily burden but the trunk was strong and could weather the storms that came with each life. I wondered why He chose a willow instead of the strong oak tree. The thought barely crossed my mind before the answer came. The oak is proud and when it falls, it falls alone. The willow though large best signifies weakness and it is in weakness and humility that one comes for help. It is only in weakness we know we need help and that is when God helps us up.

    I looked around and noticed for the first time that I was not alone. Beneath this tree were many who had traveled a path that brought them to this tree. As each one came God held out His hands and took from them all their burdens. Then when the burdens were taken He held out His arms to hold each traveler and heal the scars that each burden had etched into their life. As He held me I came to the startling realization that it was not the man at the altar I was to go and pray with it was the one in the darkness who could not see. The one who needed to know the altar was there and waiting for him too would be the tree.

MARY PENDLEBURY

PLANTING MUMS

"Wut y' doin'?" "Planting mums." "Well you ain't doin' such a good job of it". "Yesss we are!" "Well what's that over there, you can't even hardly see it?" "Oh that's Patty's mum, she don't like to been seen much so we hid her - usually she just cracks the door and yells for the kids to come in." "What about that one over there?" "Which one?" "The one in the shade… thought mums liked the sun." "Oh not Shelly's mum, she talks funny - yells at the kids a lot and the sun hurts her eyes 'specially in the morning."

"Well I think you are pretty stupid, look at these over here - you planted one upside down – one has no flowers, one has no leaves and only half of each flower. You have some explaining to do!" "Well first of all, that one planted upside down is Mia's mum. You can't see her anymore so you just have to imagine her." "The one with no flowers is Kelly's mum - we cut the flowers off 'cuz she doesn't like beautiful people or things." "Yeah, but what about the one with no leaves and only bits of flowers?" "Well that is Louise's mum because she takes away the good parts of people hoping they won't grow and she cuts the kids hair to make them feel ugly even when they aren't"

"That must be a really special one over there 'cause you haven't planted it yet." "Oh it is special alright. That's Tony's mum she can't be in the garden we are leaving her on the edge so the wind will blow her off and she will get kicked around - then there won't be any soil for her roots to grow. She doesn't like kids and we figure she will just have to try to survive like she makes her kids do, then maybe she will know what it feels like to get treated badly."

"How about that one over there, it doesn't look to bad but why do you have a stick planted with it?" "Well that's Lisa's mum. We left it like that 'cuz everybody thinks she is nice but no one knows that she uses the stick on the kids when they don't listen." "Over here is Jackie's mum". "Hey she don't look so good" Well that is because she

A FRIEND FOR ALL SEASONS

has been sick and we are going to take care of her and give her the food she needs so that she will be healthy and strong."

"This is a very curious garden you have here. There are so many mum's but not so many good looking ones." "Oh yes we do have a really nice one over here – want to see it?" "Sure." "Here it is." "Wow, this is really beautiful, can I touch it? "Yeah, go ahead!" "Hey, this ain't real!" "Oh yeah, we call that one Mrs. Perfect, we haven't met her yet but everyone says she is nice to everyone all the time."

"Well I still think you have a very strange garden but who really cares anyway?" "We care and we are going to stay here until we have finished all of our planting." "You can stay and help us if you like." "No thanks, I think you are all weird." "That's okay, nobody I know is perfect. We'll just have fun on our own. See you later." "Yeah, much later I hope." The busy little gardeners just returned to their work forgetting all about what others thought about them and what they were doing.

Before too long the street lights started coming on and one by one you could hear the various mothers calling for their children to come home… it was getting dark. All that was left was the one lone little gardener. She took some time to look at all the work she and her friends had accomplished over the course of the day. With a small sigh she went to sit on the porch to watch the sun set. She was thinking about how her mum loved the son rises but she preferred the sunsets.

Her mum loved to get up early in the morning and would wake the children up with her singing as she celebrated a new day. She would sing songs like How Great Thou Art, Morning Has Broken and a few others. At the time all the children would complain about being awakened like that but at this particular moment this little gardener would love to hear that voice again and the wonderful sound of her mum's laughter. This little gardener loved the sunsets because they were usually so beautiful and it made her feel not only happy that another day was over but all the beautiful colours gave her hope that tomorrow would be a better

MARY PENDLEBURY

day. She sat and watched the sun go down and as she did she brought her knees up to her shoulders and whispered in her heart, "Really miss you mum. Tell God thanks for the beautiful sunset."

ANGEL SOULS

It was another day in heaven where two little angels held hands as they walked and talked about so many things as they so often did. Today they were on their way to talk to God about something very important and they were very excited but also very nervous. God waited patiently for their arrival knowing full well what was on their hearts. He knew their request came with the sincerity of pure love. He watched them with a smile that only a truly loving Father could have as He watched His children stroll through His gardens. He saw their trepidation and gave them strength and courage. He saw their anxiety and gave them peace. All the while He watched each step they took and guided their steps that lead them to Him.

Now, as they stood before Him their eyes twinkled with the love that reflected from Him. They were speechless at first but He patiently waited as He always did. Their words came softly and in unison like the speech of only one. "Father, we would like to go to earth to be someone's child." God replied, "I have been waiting for you". Then He paused and as He did He looked at each one before He would tell them what they would need to know. "Each of you are truly dear to me and I will grant your request but first you must listen and hear my words and attach them to your souls." Again as if one, the angels nodded in silent approval trying to anticipate what God might say.

God spoke to their souls with warmth that soothed any fears they would have. First He told them that they would not go at the same time and would be separated to work and experience things on their own until it came time for them to need one another again. They would be put in families where there would be great strife, sorrow, pain and rejection. This, He said, would be necessary for you to do My Will. Though you are grieving, lonely, deprived and mistreated I will be with you. Then He told them that only in their souls would they know of the other before they would meet again. You will go through decades of difficult times. You will wonder if you will ever be loved but your souls will reassure one another that things will work out because My love is in you. I will teach you what you need to know and you will be given many gifts to strengthen you on your journey. My Will is that you reflect my love for you in all that you do.

   The two angels stood and listened. As they listened God was listening to the many questions that were weighing on their hearts. "I hear the questions of your heart but it will only be in time that you have them all answered". "I will tell you little more before it is time for you to go". Each angel would be born as a girl and neither of them would remember that they were angels until they returned to Him. They accepted all that God had told them because as God is pure in all things they knew that in trusting Him they would return to Him once again.

   Life on earth was very difficult. As God had said, each little girl was filled with grief, pain, sorrows beyond words and loneliness. Before the first decade had even passed each one pleaded with God to send them their friend. God knew it was not yet time for them to meet but filled their hearts with the reassurance and peace that they needed. He brought other people into their lives that would help them hold on. It wouldn't be until many of these people had returned to Heaven that He would reunite the friends. Over and over again God made parallels in their lives so that they would truly know the other when they would finally meet again. They experienced lives filled with the same kinds of people some of whom mutilated parts of their souls and spirits. Then there were some who gave them the hope and encouragement to make it through another day. These where the interim friends that God placed in their life to remind them that one day they would meet again.

   There was something special that God gave each of them that prepared them more than anything else for their reunion. Over and over again God brought people into their lives that needed their counsel, love, understanding, acceptance, care, encouragement understanding and so much more. With the gift of His love in them they were able to survive the devastation in their lives and chose to learn from their lives. They were able to give to others so much of what had not been given to them by the people in whom God had blessed with their birth. It wasn't until the second decade that they met. God had much to prepare in each of them before the time was right. They became fast friends but would be separated repeatedly as the years went by. This didn't matter in the least because the fact that they met connected them in such a way that it was as if God had attached their souls. In doing this they were able to communicate without words and knew when one needed the other. God always made a way for them to be together when it was most needed. He also made sure to continue to bring other people into their lives that were like Band-Aids until one could reach the other.

During the third decade their connection deepened to the point where they had almost made a place in their minds where they could meet and talk as if they were in the same room. They often became confused about which was the reality and which was the meeting in their minds. God works in so many ways that go beyond words. During that third decade another special thing happened. Down on earth as is witnessed all the time, so many fads come and go. There was one in particular that struck a very deep chord. A picture started circulating and showing up everywhere. It was a picture of two little angels resting on a pillow smiling like they had all the joys of a sharing a secret with God. When they saw this, it was like a reminder from God that it was Him who had brought them together again. By His grace they had been reunited to begin the next phase of their journey using all that God had brought into their lives. Since the moment that God had decided that it was time for them to meet He assisted them to use one another's experiences to help in a united force to heal their scars and help to carry one another's burdens. It was at this time that they felt blessed and loved to the depths of their souls. It was something only God could give them.

They are now living in their fourth decade. They are eternally thankful for all that they have been blessed with but most of all ever thankful that God had brought them together. As they have done since the time of their birth they are taking one day at a time. They are unknowing of how many days God has allotted to each one but each one has embedded in their hearts, minds and souls that not only will they be there for each other but so too will God.

A FRIEND FOR ALL SEASONS

THE OLD WOODEN SWING

There was a new subdivision just completed down the road and many new families had moved in one by one. It seemed the kids were moving in by the dozens. Not many played outside as they were more caught up in watching television and playing Nintendo. You just knew there were a variety of kids of all ages by the swarms that inched their way to the bus stop each morning at eight a.m.

Then there were two who were different. They decided to explore the area surrounding their new home. Wondering the streets, they found a pathway that led to a hideaway unknown to any new comer. They just had to see what was down this path and followed it for what seemed like hours to them. They were richly rewarded for their efforts. To their amazement they came upon an opening and saw a very old oak tree. That was not all that was there. The grass was a rich green and came up to their knees. There were a variety of wild flowers and they stopped at once to pick some to take home with them. It was like a paradise that could scarce be taken in all at once. They were like one in their thought as together they looked up and over to that very old oak tree... Each looked at the other like they had just found gold. Hanging from the very old oak tree was a swing. Just one swing with the wooden seat suspended from the tree buy rope that was almost as old as the tree itself.

This was an opportunity that could not be passed up. Simultaneously they ran skipped and jumped their legs scarcely able to keep up with the thought of who would get there first to have a turn on that swing. They reached the swing at the same time both breathless but not wanting to have to wait their turn. After a short staring contest of decision they came to a compromise. "Hey, this swing is big enough for both of us". The swing was pretty high off the ground but they struggled together to get up there like two birds on a single perch. Feeling very proud of their accomplishment they looked at one another beaming with delight and laughing. Laughing just because… Now they would have to figure out just how they would work this so that they could get the swing moving without one of them falling off. After a few minutes that problem was also solved. Once again working as a team they pushed off. The giggling stopped for a short time as each one was catapulted into another realm.

They were like birds in flight… enjoying the feeling of cutting through the air. In their minds and bodies flying through the mild breeze that was blowing. Imaging a million things like taming a hurricane, floating on the clouds, being on top of the world. Then one says to the other… " I know, let's pretend we are on a ship in a storm, let's swing sideways and see how high we can go without hitting the tree. And once again they worked together slowing but surely changing directions… leaning into each side, one leg at a time… creating the sensation of riding the waves.

This went on for hours; they just couldn't get enough of the world they were creating. Cocooned in their own reality, a universe of their own. They began to tire and together sat on the swing and just swayed back and forth slowly. Letting their legs and feet be cooled by the grass below after long since kicking off the shoes that opened the door to the other realm. Drifting on the swing they talked about so many things. They talked about what was happening at home and about their hopes and dreams and all the things that made them laugh. "Know what? We should keep this place a secret and not tell anybody at all" "Just you and me can come here whenever we want to". "Yeah, let's not tell anyone!" " This is just so cool it's like a secret hiding place". "Hey next time we can bring a lunch or something". "Yeah, that is way cool, let's do that!"

The sun had reached a point in the sky which left them a little saddened at the realization that it was time to head back. " We really should head back, I have to get supper made and the kids will be home soon". "Yeah, I have a pile of laundry to get done and I really dread the thought of that." "Yeah I hear you, we really should head back". And so the two adventurers headed back to their homes and the reality that each one held. Each one would keep that promise to return not only to the place where there sat

A FRIEND FOR ALL SEASONS

waiting for them the old wooden swing, but to a time when things were so much simpler. Returning often to that place where life was restored and where every hope and dream was within their grasp with every swing to- and- fro then left to right.

MARY PENDLEBURY

MEDUSA

    We have a tree in our yard that we call Medusa. It's dead in reality but has created a new life in the sense that we have come up with a lifetime of creative ideas on how we should remove it. We call it Medusa because it stands there staring at us with that multitude of dead branches wildly hanging over head like the wild snaky hair of Medusa. Medusa stands grey but strong. It has seen a lot of storms but only once had to withstand the strike of lightning that severed a couple of limbs.

    Yes, we have come up with many ideas to remove Medusa- scaling its heights with spikes in our shoes… a saw in one hand and chain saw in the other… prepared to do battle from the top to the ground. We've thought of rigging up ropes anchored possibly to the building out back and persuading its decent to the ground by notching it with an axe. Then there was the idea to wash it out with the hose or create some other "natural" disaster that would be covered by insurance in the event that we miscalculated and it accidentally landed on the house. One time it was rittled with bullets from a gun and Medusa mocked us by spitting them back.

    It has been a tourist attraction to blue jays, woodpeckers, squirrels, and blackbirds to name a few. All intent on using it as a place to rest, a place to make noise of as just a means to get to another tree. Medusa is left undaunted standing there staring, mocking, and refusing to fall. Everyday we sit out eyeing it back – plotting our schemes, measuring and angling potential falls. Another day comes and another day goes. Medusa stands. It has become somewhat of a conversation piece with the neighbours who offer suggestions and voice their concerns. Nothing changes – Medusa stands.

    Then we are back at the drawing board, trying to find new ways to solve the problem. But how do you solve a problem like Medusa? The sparkle returned to our eyes. Medusa would become a totem pole. We will carve, chisel, and saw… until the task is complete.

There would be carvings of light bulbs to represent the many ideas we had come up with - sculptures of the various animals and birds who spent time there. There would be carvings of people laboring with sweat in an attempt to conquer the mighty Medusa. We would make it a memorial to all the storms that failed in their attacks.

There are so many things that would make our totem pole truly unique. When we are wearied with the task completed we will paint it with vibrant colors in celebration of our labours. We can paint it with vibrant colours just so it be such and eye sore- and because grey just doesn't go with anything else in the yard. We will rejoice at a job well done and pat ourselves on the back for our ingenuity and creativity. We will come to peace with the fact that Medusa is here to stay though changed in appearance still standing strong.

Another day will come and another day will go and we will sit outside as we have done so many times before. We will stare at Medusa and Medusa will stare back. As we are savoring our victory Medusa will lean then rock and fall to the ground once again having the last word. Mocking us again… Medusa will fall

A DAY WITH LANCE

The snow wafted down covering everything in sight. The road glistened like a million stars in the sky. It was cold and windy but even that would not deter them from making the long trip in their short school bus. Everyone pitched in to clear the snow from around the bus. It was an arduous task for most but this group went about their business with great expectation. It was a special day for the whole class. They had talked about this day for two weeks.

Miss Diane had explained how they were going on an outing to meet someone who used to be in her class. She explained how he was special just like them. With every detail their eyes grew to the size of saucers. It came to be the highlight of the previous two weeks. She told them how they too could grow up to be just like Lance. She told them how when Lance was young like them he rode in the short school bus too and every morning he came to school with oatmeal on his face. He didn't mean to, he would say, but it was his favorite food and he couldn't start the day without it. Every morning Miss Diane had to take Lance into the boy's room and wash his face. And every morning they did just that and Lance would come out of the boy's room so proud of himself wearing a big toothless grin.

Lance was not the most coordinated boy in class. He was on the chubby side and was forever running into things or simply tripping over seemingly nothing. Sometimes he just couldn't get his arms and legs flailing the same way and would trip over his own feet. Other times he was clumsy because he was so distracted by the little blonde girl in his class. He followed her everywhere and could rarely be found at his desk where he belonged. Miss Diane told the class how she taught Lance how to skip in hopes of helping him to improve his balance. He took to the skipping with great pride hoping to show everyone in his class how fancy he could be. Every time the blonde haired girl would look at him he would get all tangled in the rope and turn wonderful shades of red. Miss Diane thought skipping would be a good place to begin because Lance already spent a lot of his time walking on his toes, springing up and down as he walked.

The children were eager to hear everything they could about Lance. This created the atmosphere of anticipation for their class outing. She encouraged them to come up with questions of their own to ask Lance when they met him. They practiced over and over again how they would behave, how they would talk and who would ask which questions. Now the day was here. They were going t see someone who had become almost bigger than life over the past two weeks. In no time at all the snow was cleared from off the bus. Miss Diane knew how excited they were but knew it was best to take some more time as they started the drive to review some rules and have them sing songs to help them settle down for the ride.

An hour later they arrived outside the place where Lance worked. Each had now migrated to the side of the bus where they could see more. Every window on the right side of the bus had become a collage of hands and faces eager to catch a glance of their hero. Lance saw the bus pull up and went outside to greet the visitors. He said hello to Miss Diane and all she could see was the chubby little boy who used to come to class each day with oatmeal on his face and a skipping rope tangled about his feet. It took Miss Diane a minute to come back to the present. The class had suddenly become very quiet - overwhelmed with excitement and nervousness. Donald began to cry because he had just filled his pants and the smell was bad. That always happened when he was really nervous. Miss Diane was prepared and took out the change of clothing asking Lance where she could take Donald and clean him up. She asked Lance if he would mind staying with the class until she returned and he proudly complied. At first everyone was still very quiet so he wasn't expecting any problems. He introduced himself to the class and explained that he really liked working at the Big Gym because it gave him a lot of time to practice his skipping. It also gave him the chance to use a lot of new machines to make himself stronger. Lance didn't want to have to explain how every machine worked but he thought that if he had his new friends ask some questions maybe it would make things easier for him to know where to begin.

Lance asked the class if they had any questions. The silence was suffocating. As Lance backed up he hooked himself on a machine and almost fell. This was the ice-breaker that sent the class into hysterics. Then from the back of the crowd came a booming voice. "How come you are so short?" Then another… "Do you still like oatmeal?" "Do you lift big weights?" "Do you still ride the small school bus?" "How do you work this machine?" "Can I try this machine?" Before Lance knew it the class had dispersed itself throughout the gym eager to try everything in sight. Swinging from everything that looked interesting. Some ran to the bikes anticipating a heated race only to be let down with the realization that the bikes didn't have a back wheel and wouldn't be going anywhere. Lance didn't know where to go first. His mind was racing.…All he could do was stand there and wave his arms up and down hoping it would ease the stress of the situation and help him to gather his thoughts.

Just then Miss Diane returned with Donald and looking at Lance she once again saw that little boy who in one moment could stand proud as a peacock and in the next moment be broken by embarrassment turning red and waving his arms. Miss Diane took a moment to touch him on the shoulder to bring him back to the present. She lost Donald's grip and he had taken off to join the others. Miss Diane took a deep breath and as she released it she loudly clapped her hands and called the children to gather in a circle. Usually she only had to do this once but today was different. She repeated the order five times before everyone had assembled and before some degree of order was restored. Only then could the visit continue. Each child calmed down and asked the questions they had been practicing. After half and hour or more the visit would be winding up. Before they left everyone gathered in a quiet room to thank Lance for letting them come for a visit and then have their snack break. Lance stayed for snack too because he needed to sit and have a bowl of oatmeal. Just as he had done so many times in the past, he ate too fast and left with oatmeal clinging to his face. This endeared him to the children once again and reminded them that just like Lance they could go on to do great things.

   Everyone said their good-byes and Lance stood outside watching as the bus pulled away. The collage of faces beaming in the afterglow of their visit with Lance. When the bus was out of site Lance returned to his job but just as he had done when he was a boy – he didn't stay at his desk but rather made a bee- line for the little blonde he spotted at the back of the gym. He only tripped once on his way back to impress her. All she saw was that silly smirk that was his trade mark opener. No witty one liners this time though because before he could say a word the little blonde remarked… "Gee, Lance I really liked your friends, do they come here often?" He wasn't sure what to say and before he knew it he had once again turned red and his arms began to flap. He turned on his heels hoping to bow out of the situation gracefully only to once again hook himself on a machine… trying desperately to be cool as he pulled together the tear that extended his pocket to his knee.

MARY PENDLEBURY

REBEL ROUSER

It was quieter at the gym them it usually was. People mulling around just doing their thing. The odd grunt was heard from those macho guys that have to let you know that they are lifting more than they should. Other than that things were pretty normal. The music was playing as usual. Nothing in particular stood out. Then the time came for the arrival of work out twins. They had come to do their "time" and leave half satisfied. A few people noticed they had come in and they said their hellos then went about their business.

As they chatted about what they would do next, something changed. Their attention was held captive by the song that was just starting. That look came over their faces that let you know it could only be one thing…. Their heads began to twitch and their legs were ready to go… and when they could take it no more the whole gym heard it… "IT'S POLKA TIME!!!" One of them grabs the arm of the lady in the paisley workout clothes. She was ready to go….YAHOOOO!!! There was no stopping her now. It should be mentioned that this polka dance was a time- honored tradition (about two weeks old) but not everyone appreciated it the same way.

There was Tony… his face dropped and his eyes were rolling back in his head. "I HATE THIS SONG!" Well that was all the twins needed to hear. He was in for it now. They headed right for him and spun him around a few times. His enthusiasm was lame at best… To the twins this was good physiotherapy for his recently injured leg. To Tony it was more painful than having both legs amputated. He was caught up in the swirling again before being left to stew in the aftermath of his perceived torture. The twins and the paisley lady were in for the long haul despite the fact that Tony was waiting for the paisley lady to return so he could finish their training session.

A FRIEND FOR ALL SEASONS

At long last the song ended and things returned to the somewhat normal calm that existed before "the song" came on. Once again the gym's occupants droned on with their workouts and once again you could hear the odd grunt from the macho men. "That's okay" said the one twin with that sheepish smile… "We can do it all again tomorrow, I have lots of polka left in me yet!" And off they went to finish off the workout that began as it had everyday in the gym that had no appreciation for the finer things in life. The gym that was filled with those who deem that to be different was the greatest faux pas of al and that life should always go on as it had before. Things would never be the same at that gym again… The twins broke that mold for good. Although everyone appeared to be appalled by the twins actions… if you looked very closely you could see the grins and if you listened closely there were other rebels there who just couldn't get the song out of their heads. The song had ended but the humming lingered in the minds and mouths of those who knew deep in their hearts that they were every bit as much of a rebel. And the day went on but it was different now and so were the people who had witnessed the time -honored tradition of Polka Time at the BigGym.

MARY PENDLEBURY

NOT JUST ANOTHER CARDIO CLASS

We were all assembled prepared to do battle. It was here that we came to empty ourselves of the stress of the week. Our instructor had the experience well under control but her need for spontaneity was about to rule the day. The class would take so many unexpected turns but she had a room full of willing participants. The music began and the warm up was about to start. "Let's begin by doing some stretches". Each one in the class straining to do their best. We warmed up our shoulders, our arms and our legs. As the tempo of the music picked up so did our anticipation of what was to come. Usually we just used a skipping rope, punching bags and boxing gloves but today they brought out tap shoes as well. Today the class was not called kick boxing but rather for today it would be called Karioke… Tapping to Kick Boxing Classics. The music echoed in our head, as did the words… "Be aggressive… be…be… be aggressive!"

Our instructor was no longer going by the name of Michelle … today she would be Mich-Elle of the Amazon Women. The floor and walls were no longer a room but had become "Thunder Dome". We went through our moves… Snap… Punch… Hook… Tap… Tap… Upper Cut… Snap… Punch, hook, kick, snap…Strike…Tap… Tap… Tap… Jumping Jacks were always difficult but now they were replaced with intricate dance moves that would give Gene Kelly and Gregory Hines reason to worry. "Again…" she said " Snap … Punch… Hook…" Then the fun began, not only would we be kicking to the side but tap dancing on the walls at the same time. What a rush!

Skipping took on a new meaning… The tapping was in unison broken only by the odd entanglement in a rope. All the while each person in turn took to karioke. Sometimes we all sang together to get a read on our endurance while increasing our cardio out-put. At last it was time to do a little work on the bags. Again the tapping persisted as we made our way around the bag. Clickity, click, clickity, clickity, click – jab, snap, kick, snap, punch, snap, snap, clickity, clickity, click. Amidst the tapping and singing you could hear the odd cry of "Hit it 'til it bleeds" or the ring of something resembling the scream of karate kid ready to attack. Between sets we raced around Thunder Dome… running and tapping… side to side… this only to be broken by the tapping on the wall followed by a back flip. Clickity … click… clickity… click we were on a role.

Time always passed so quickly in that class and once again it had come time to wind down. That was always hard to do but today more so because of the extra adrenaline rush. The only thing prompting us to let go was the incredible stench that emanated from every hand. It wasn't just your everyday smell of perspiration but rather, collectively it smelled as though something had died in the room. The newest members were appalled but the rest of us knew that death resided on the inside of the boxing gloves. To the untrained eye, the class appeared to be over but not to those in the know. The final act of participation in this class was the fifty-yard dash that took you to the ladies room in an attempt to sterilize your hands. Everyone was "on their mark" and ready to go.

As everyone dashed out the door, the room continued to echo with the sounds of Thunder Dome. The equipment had been returned to its resting-place and Mich-Elle of the Amazon Women returned to reality as she prepared to drift off to her continued duties as personal trainer. It was another great day for cardio and the vote was unanimous… Karioke Tapping to Kick Boxing Classics was a keeper. No longer would Cardio Kick boxing be enough for anyone who had been to Thunder Dome.

HOT AND COLD FLASHES

You think you have problems? Well not to worry you're all alone and no one cares about your pain. No thank you for sharing. If things don't get any better I am going to throw a car at someone. Have you uttered any of these remarks? Then you probably have PMS. Most people have heard of PMS but not when it stands for Permanent Metabolic Screw-up! Yes, you heard it right. Recent research suggests that it accompanies another lesser-known disorder by the name of C.F.I.D.S (not to be confused with Chronic Fatigue Immune Dysfunction Syndrome). This disorder goes by the name of Certifiable Frenzied Internal Deterioration and Shutdown. Also know as M.E (Mutiny in its Entirety).

This disease is enough to flap the greatest minds ever to work on the likes of PMS and Menopause. It's like nothing they have ever seen before. Hands like ice, toes on fire, goosebumps on one side of your and nothing on the other side. The outer skin is cool and clammy while your internal organs are raging like the finest Hawaiian volcanoes.

You wake up feeling closer to normal than you have in a long time and start the day thinking that you are the greatest thing since sliced bread – and then it happens. You bend over to pick up a few crumbs off the floor and WHAM! The floor around you begins to melt around you… the heat you are throwing off could roast a 30 lb. Turkey to perfection in under an hour. You are sure it will pass at any moment so you tread lightly and touch as little as possible because it is getting expensive replacing all the heat damaged articles in your home. Fifteen minutes pass and you give in to the heat exhaustion and dehydration.

You don't think you will make it upstairs before you faint or start a fire but you do your best. AHHHHH!!!! – At last you have changed into something resembling shorts and a tank top and you are praying to stave off another episode of spontaneous combustion. You are still sweating profusely but it seems so trivial. You wave your arms about in an attempt to circulate some cool air around your body. You think, this is great it's working but what is that noise. Clunk! Clunk… clunk and the nightmare continues as all the sweat is freezing and now as you wave your arms your body is throwing off ice cubes. Now your body is defying science by doing your impression of sauna on the rocks. Where will it end…? Now only half of your body is throwing off ice cubes and the other half is almost at room temperature. If only you hadn't left your outfit idea laying on the drawing board. You know the one. The lovely two piece co-ordinating sundress snowsuit you meant to finish up last year. It would really come I handy now especially with all the accessories you had. The thermal mini skirt/full length zip up the feet-warming blanket. The toque industrial strength sweat absorber. The sandals and purse with the heat detector sprinkler systems. And my favorite the thermal rap that retained whatever temperature was coming off your body and storing it to compensate for the severe unannounced body temperature change.

All these thoughts keep going through your head each time you have to run upstairs to change again… Maybe I have PTSD – no not PostTraumatic Stress disorder, but Post Thermonuclear Searing Discoloration. I wonder if the smoke detectors are working - Have the fire extinguishers been serviced … If I have to run up these stairs one more time I am going to be a Weeble. Weebles wobble because their legs fell off – or something like that. I wonder if anyone can possibly understand that each shift in temperature has it's own sound. When the heat wave comes… it sounds like the strobe lights in a bad sci-fi movie and especially like the parts when you have that glowing blob of alien ooze. Then the sound changes to something resembling the snow of a television with really bad reception.

Just as you are sorting though the vast array of thoughts that are sweeping through your head a stab of reality hits. Two very dangerous thoughts… Oh no, I am entering the PMS zone – someone is going to die… or at least have severe injuries inflicted on their being if I don't make it through today. The second bite of reality is that the menopause monster is whispering in your ear with all the charm of the big bad wolf… "I'm coming to get you" Why is it such a shock to people when they learn how many women ended up in asylums as they entered menopause.

   The day drones on and you desperately pray for your brain and body to call a truce. In the best interest of your family and all mankind this madness has to stop. You are a great asset to those around you. You can keep them warm while at the same time providing an endless supply of ice for their drinks. But how much fun is it to entertain when you are feeling like the Tasmanian devil and don't have a thing to wear.

HOUSE OF HORRORS

She raced out of the house fearing she would be late for that of so important appointment. Steadfast she watched the road to avoid "the drivers". They were grouped I the same group as everyone on the read but they were the ones that could only drive you crazy. One last left turn and she was there. She locked the vehicle as she made her way toward the open door. Walking into the light isn't always what you think.

Politely they welcomed her as she sat down to read. Occasionally she peeked over the top of her magazine to reassure herself that she hadn't been forgotten. Before she knew it her name was called and she was escorted to the back. She was barely seated again before a flood of water and suds clouded her head. The woman kept making small talk with her but she could comprehend nothing with her ears full of water and her neck feeling like it was about to snap. Quickly a towel is placed around her head and once again she is escorted to a new chair.

"Yes, yes" the lady says, " I remember well- you're the one with #7 blonde- Looks so nice on you!" "Yes, yes no problem- you'll be done in no time- I have your card here with very exact instructions." She was somehow not comforted by those words she had heard a million times before. The first application begins and foolishly she lets down her guard and begins to relax. "Oh yes, this will look so nice on you. You will be happy."

Time goes by and it is time for the rinse and test… Her legs are buckling and her nerves on alert. The revelation was not good she knew she was in trouble. "Not to worry, we aren't done yet". She almost bites her tongue off – She sees what is happening. "Noooo….I want blonde hair not brown!" The internal screaming begins and the panic is blurring her vision. The toner was next and no hope was in sight. Now we are looking at a color somewhere between purple and red. Actually she was seeing red; no one is sure what the actual color of the hair is. "No problem- we can fix that…let's start again."

Knowing she is in the danger zone and the point of no return she sits back down… Her eyes are darting from side to side and she desperately wants to put both hands on top of her head to stave off the explosion she knows is inevitable. As she raises her hands she eyes her friend peering through the window and her and waves pleadingly for her to come in. Her eyes are pleading – "Help me, I'm descending into hell". Her friend runs to get some water in hopes of quelling the heat, then takes a seat next to her and gauges the torment at hand.

Round two just completed it is time for the unveiling – "**ORANGE HAIR! NOOOOO… I WANT BLONDE… HOW DIFFICULT CAN THAT BE?**" "The woman's voice drones into her rage… "But I followed the card exactly, I don't know what happened… I don't know what went wrong. But…I…I…I can fix it". She looks to her friend as the lady leaves to get a new bottle of magic. She is an 8.8 earthquake coming to the surface. Her friend holds on tight because she knows a bumpy ride doesn't begin to explain the terror to come. The lady returns and nicely, in a quivering sort of way, asks her to put her head back as she begins again. Around and around the mixture in the bottle goes. The friend just can't keep her eyes in her head and sits with a stare that rivaled and Marty Feldman act. The eyes have pretty much launched themselves from their sockets.

Again the lady's voice cracks the screaming silence. "Time to rinse!" People only sound that high pitched when they are dangling from the end of a rope. Towel atop her head they return to the mirror to reveal – what? Yes, now we have blonde and white concentric circles. The lady nicely bleached every ounce of colour from her hair in a massive array of halos and she wasn't feeling anything close to an angel at that point.

Does she start to cry now or allow the lady one more chance? She knows what she ought to do but she can't leave looking the way she does but doesn't want a criminal record for what she would like to do, so she sits down for round three. By this time she is getting a very numb bum because this simple appointment is into it's fourth hour. Once again the color is applied and all the steps have been completed. What she is left with is something resembling what is suppose to be blonde with evidence remaining of the bulls-eye effect that wasn't going to be easy to miss.

Now she is sure that there is an unspoken conspiracy in the works. For two years now she has done battle of the blonde. When she finally gets someone who knows what they are doing, they either get sick or fired and another scrimmage ensues in her attempts to find someone who can keep her blonde. She never knows what she will leave with but one thing is for certain…. If she has another day like this she will have no choice but to shave her head and begin wearing wigs. She has gone from black to blonde to sandy-brownish-blonde to strawberry blond to three different shades of relatively acceptable blonde to who knows what. Her friends have renamed her Diane and the hair of many colours.

Once again this brave soldier ventures out into the unknown. And once again she seems to have found someone who is willing and able to help her. But it is an arduous journey and somehow she finds the strength to go on. For this she deserves accolades. She isn't so sure – more than anything she want peace – a truce with the head of hair that defies explanation or reason. It was a simple request – She wanted to be blonde but more than anything she just got the blahs, which is how the whole thing started.

MARY PENDLEBURY

I'VE LOST MY MIND

Good grief, I've done it again, I've lost my mind. I know I had it a minute ago because I just… Well I know I went upstairs to get something and next thing I knew, it was gone. No not the stairs… I'm sure they are still there.

I've got the stares…. Where was I going? Why am I brining the jar of jam up to the attic? Oh yes, I remembered while I was making a sandwich that I needed to refinish that old dresser for Jan. She always did like jam sandwiches. Why is the dog staring at me and why does she keep following me all over the house? Perhaps I should just sit here a minute and finish my snack. Hey this isn't my sandwich – I think I just broke a tooth. I am sure that wasn't a raspberry seed! And why is the dog still staring at me? Maybe I should get a drink of water that may help.

Okay, I came out to the garage to get something. What was it? Oh there is the can of paint I was looking for. I should touch up that baseboard while I am thinking of it. Where did those paint brushes go…? I know I put them right here. Maybe I left them upstairs… I should go look now while I am thinking of it. It will only take a second. Darn it! The phone… don't hang up I am almost there! "Yes, hello Mrs. Strechmarkstein, your children are in my yard." "Yes, I will them home." "No, I am sorry I can't talk right now I am trying to get a few things done before my husbands comes home." "Yes, I will send your children home." "Yes, thank you. You have a nice day too!" "Bye for now." "Yes, bye-bye" "Yes, I will call you later. Have a nice day now!" So many interruptions, how will I get anything done. Better go and send the children home. Hmmmmm… they were in the back yard… Perhaps they have gone around front. I should go and see. Oh great, the mail is here. I'll take that in before I forget.

What was it I wanted in the garage. Maybe if I go back inside I will remember. Must go to the bathroom before I do anything else. Darn! End of the roll, I'll have to go back upstairs and get some

A FRIEND FOR ALL SEASONS

more. "Yes, Derek!" "What is it?" "You can't find your Gameboy?" "It's on your dresser"… "ARRRRRGH!" "Here it is next to your Walkman." "I am going to go and lay down for a few minutes so please try and be quiet for me." "Thank you."

Four hours later…

"Oh, hi Hun!" "What did I do today?" "Aaaaaaah… well I…" "Why are you laughing?" "Hhhuh?" "Would you please repeat that?" "You came in the garage and found my glass of water… You found the dog dish sitting on the living room table next to the dog who was staring at you… Then what?" You came up to see me and noticed rolls of toilet paper on the stairs…. When you got to the top of the stairs you noticed the attic door was open and the light was on. When you went up to shut off the light you found a jar of jam and a sandwich. Then when you came down form the attic there was a can of paint in the hall?" "Felt like I had done a lot today and I am still tired and hungry too!" "Yes, the mail is right here!" "I left what in the mail box?" "I have been looking for those paint brushes all day!" "Who called?" "OOOOPS! Did her children get home alright?" "Ooooh Noooo, they just came in when she was on the phone with you… wondering why they weren't home hours ago? "Geeeesh!" "Honey, can you find just one thing for me – I have lost my mind. I think I had it this morning when I woke up but now I can't even be certain of that.

MARY PENDLEBURY

IN THE TRENCHES

At long last... the opportunity to finally do some gardening. We had so much fun choosing the plants and deciding where everything would go. There would be hours and hours of fun for the two of us. We moved bushes, pruned trees, turned the soil and added another area to place some of these precious plants. The excitement was heightened by the addition of rose bushes, azaleas and other small shrub-like plants that would be used as ground cover. Just imagining what the finished product would be was enough to help us continue in our endeavors.

Then the days and weeks would pass as we enjoyed anew with each day the work of our backs and hands... shovels and trowels. Stepping out like parents to see how the young ones were doing... did they have enough water... do they need more food. Then simply enjoying the vibrant colors and wonder-filled smells that emanated from our surroundings. All this was enriched by the warm summer days, which held the occasional breeze that cooled our brows. It was one such day that beckoned us to the gardens to see how everyone was doing. The wave petunias had readily expressed their gratitude by filling in one of the new areas in the front yard. Waving in jubilation for their new- found freedom and the space to expand their roots and multiply their blooms. The impatients were looking a little weary but sprang back to life with a cool drink of water. The alyssum boarder around the front gave a splendid contrast to the array of color in the geraniums the holly and the evergreens not to mention the exquisite color of the planters to each side of the front door.

Seeing the success of the front yard brought great expectations of what the back had in store for us. We would sit out on the patio furniture and have some tea before continuing on our tour. Well the tea would not be finished because our mission drew us away. Some of the azaleas were looking questionable but most were doing well. They too would be given some water in hopes that they would recover. We split up as one went to see how the vegetable garden was coming along while the other checked in on the roses and surrounding terrain. Bending over to snatch a daring weed from between the tomato plants was simple enough but I had never heard a plant scream before. My mistake, it wasn't the plant at all… it had come from over near the roses… "Oh my god… what are they?" "Something is attacking the roses!" "Oh my god… eeeeewwww…. Get out of here!"… I had never seen a dance done quite like that before but I knew what it was. It was the "This is so gross it is making my skin crawl dance… the skin crawl that sends the skin from your toes racing towards your ears". "Quick, help me get these things off the roses". Together we attempted to flick these bugs off with our fingers… this progressed to swinging at them with fly swatters and tennis racquets. It wasn't working; the plants were under siege.

We would have to think this through… "Stand back, I'll get the spray". That didn't work either. These bugs were coming in from everywhere landing like paratroopers invading our garden. We would have to bring in the heavy artillery. "Base one to base two … do you read me over?"… "Base two to base one…I read… over." "Base one to base two…pull back we need to get cover… Over…" We retreated but only long enough to prepare for battle. Within an hour we were back… helmets on our heads made of old flower-pots and camouflaged with the tree prunings from the previous weeks. Flack jackets made of raincoats and bb-guns in hand we headed back to the front line. We crawled on our bellies across the lawn and up the hill to the front lines ever careful not to be seen.

We did our research… these were Japanese beetles and they were not about to give up those roses until they had them completed destroyed… even then they may still continue to nibble on them a little more. We were sure we had not been seen in our approach but perhaps we had been deceived. We had been so careful in making sure we had prepared in every way but somehow the word got out that we were coming. Thinking back on it now it may have been that in our exuberance to get the job done we forgot to change out of our neon pink and green flip-flops and into our combat runners. That's not important now we had a mission to do and we were bound and determined to see it through. Yes, we had the little buggers in the cross hairs and ready to fire.... It was like we had been bitten by the fires of hell. Those little buggers had sent in the infantry... we were being flanked on all sides by the fire ant infantry from "Left-of - Hill". They were well known in the area but to our knowledge at that time we had already exterminated them weeks ago. Apparently they had gone underground and were just sitting in wait for a moment such as this.

"Base one to base two... they got me... over"... Base one to base two do you read? over" "Base two to base one... I read... let's get the hell out of here!...over" Base one to base two...copy that... we will have to head back to the garden center... pull back now... Over".... "Base two to base one.... Copy that ...over" We pulled back, wounded but not defeated. We would head back to base to bring in some more sprays and do and air strike. Back to the gardening center we went and purchased the spray that would do the trick. It was formulated specifically for this problem. Our bravery had returned because along with the air strike on the Japanese beetles we brought a little extra to take care of the infantry. We each ascended the hill, sprays in hand... One starting from "Left-of-Hill" the other starting from ground zero... the beetle camp. We covered the entire area with the precision of ace sprayers... missing nothing, double spraying anything that looked suspicious. And when we were done we retreated but not before standing on top of the hill and hands on hips announcing that our work here was done. Then back we returned to the tea that had been sitting far too long. We refreshed the cups and sat out on the patio furniture with that whimsical look of shear satisfaction on our faces... "Let's just see them try anything like that again ... the little buggers... cheers to us!" "A job well done!". The battle was over at least for now and that was all that mattered. We could now once again enjoy the fruits of our labors for what remained of the season. Next year was too far off to worry about on such a nice day. It would be left alone until it was time to arrive and here were two who would be better equipped to handle it all.

A FRIEND FOR ALL SEASONS

ISBN 1412019887-5